IT WAS GREAT TO SAY HELLO TO...

A Curious Radio Host's Conversations With Actors, Authors, and Newsmakers

It Was Great To Say Hello To...

Ed Kalegi

Paperback ISBN: 9781950544547
EBook ISBN: 9781950544516

Rand-Smith Publishing
Rand-Smith LLC

First Printing, 2024

Contents

Introduction

It all started with a $7.95 walkie-talkie and a 9-volt battery.

***

I began to scratch my radio itch at an early age. When I was ten years old, I set up my own radio station in my bedroom. (Full disclosure: it wasn't some sort of pirate radio station, so anyone reading this at the Federal Communications Commission can immediately relax and stand down.) It was one $7.95 Radio Shack walkie-talkie with the "talk" button taped down into place so the microphone was always on, broadcasting with the flame-throwing super-charged power of one 9-volt battery. Unfortunately, my bedroom radio station was ratings challenged from the start, as any audience was limited to some kid walking within 150 feet of my house using the exact same brand of walkie-talkie. I read live commercials that I had transcribed from the radio, I played songs from my cassette recorder, and I talked about the news, sports, and weather. I even interviewed some of my friends. I was instantly hooked.

My high school years allowed me to fully understand and express my personality as a member of the drama department at Bishop George Ahr/St. Thomas Aquinas High School in Edison, NJ. It was the most advanced high school drama department in the area, taught and directed by Gordon Inverno, Jr. It was an amazing learning experience; most importantly, I learned the art of timing and presentation. It also allowed me the opportunity to perform at the Bucks County Playhouse in New Hope, PA, which to this day remains a highly regarded regional theater.

My college years were spent at Rutgers University, where I was finally allowed to be on the air at the student radio station, WRSU-FM. At first, I wanted to work in sports, so my freshman year was spent doing a weekly fifteen-minute Friday evening sportscast on *The Matt Pinfield Show*. Matt was a champion of 1980s alternative music and became a popular and influential MTV personality in the 1990s. Today, he is heard on KLOS in Los Angeles. I was also a play-by-play announcer for a couple of Rutgers basketball games. My other responsibility was to occasionally host *Knightline,* the WRSU post-game call-in show. During one snowy night of my sophomore year, my collegiate radio future changed dramatically.

Knightline had run late because a very early December snowstorm kept the overnight student DJ from getting to the studio in time for the show. This was in 1986, before voice tracking and automation technology. In those days, college radio was live or wasn't at all. My co-host that evening, Mike Emanuel, who today works for Fox News, needed to leave around midnight. The DJ for the next shift said he could get a train to New Brunswick and arrive around 2:00 AM. So, there I was: alone, hosting a call-in show after an early season blowout loss by the Rutgers men's basketball team, which meant no one wanted to call in and discuss the disappointing outcome. Instead of droning on about the game, I asked the audience: "You know what? *Knightline* is done for the night, so let's do this: what is the absolute worst part of being stuck inside on a Saturday night during a blizzard?" Immediately, one call came in, then another, and another, and they kept calling for over two hours from all over Central Jersey. It was my first real talk show. It was an exhilarating rush that I can still tap into as I write this. I knew that, even though it was the first time I had done this, I was doing something I was meant to do. At that moment, I found my own personal definition of the word surreal.

A few days later, I found a note in my student mailbox asking me to stop by WLBS, the other student radio station at Rutgers. At this point, WLBS was a small AM station heard only on the Livingston campus of Rutgers in Piscataway, across the river from New Brunswick. When I visited, the station manager said he heard the impromptu blizzard talk show and asked if I would be interested in hosting a morning show there. They wanted a typical 1980s morning format: fun conversation with some music tossed in. He also mentioned they were on the verge of partnering with a local high school with an FM license but broadcasting only two hours a day. The rest of the broadcast day would be ours. I would have the morning show as many days a week as I wanted, and I would also immediately be the sports director and provide the play-by-play for *all* the Rutgers football and basketball games I wanted. That meant I'd have my own morning show and my own sports department. Goodbye, WRSU, and hello, WLBS.

The next three years were some of the most memorable of my life. *The Entertainment Extravaganza* aired mornings from 6:00 until 10:00 and, during the final year, also at night from 10:00 to midnight, when, yes, we did jack up the transmitter and boost the signal into New York City. (Uh oh, I guess the FCC really can come after me now.) We did scripted comedy, took phone calls, played the latest Madonna, Michael Jackson, and Bruce Springsteen hits, and had an incredible time. We played the music that was popular at the time, songs that were also heard locally on Z100 and WPLJ, not the obscure and sometimes weird music heard on college radio. It was an ensemble show, and fellow Rutgers students, including Tim, another Ed, Mindy, Brian, Jenny, and Scott, helped me develop as an air personality and helped create memories that are as fresh and meaningful today as they were then. Comedian Gilbert Gottfried stopped by the studio one morning as he was performing on campus later that night. Consumer advocate and former Green Party Presidential Candidate Ralph Nader paid a visit as well. They were my first celebrity interviews. Rutgers men's assistant basketball coach Jeff Van Gundy, who went on to coach the

New York Knicks and enjoyed a long run as the lead analyst for NBA broadcasts on ESPN and ABC, had a recurring segment on the show.

WLBS soon moved from AM to FM and became WRLC, which broadcasts today from Rutgers University as "The Core" 90.3 RLC-WVPH-FM. I remain very proud that our show helped establish and build what today, all these years later, is a thriving and award-winning community radio station. While some colleges and universities are returning their FM broadcast licenses to the FCC and eliminating traditional student radio stations, Rutgers University maintains two FM student radio stations. That's a very good thing. By the way, my son is currently part of WRSU at Rutgers. He's been the Program Director, Assistant Sports Director, and Sports Director.

Now, this is where the story gets a bit confusing, not for you but for me. I decided to take the so-called safe route and accept a position as a branch manager at a local marketing company. I fought against my heart and followed the advice of some around me who said going into radio was a bad career move. At Rutgers, I had even gotten past the first audition to be accepted into the acting program at the Mason Gross School of the Arts. Still, I never pursued it further as I heard things like: "What, do you think you're gonna be in a movie someday?" and "Get a job with a good company, and they'll take care of you for the rest of your life." Ultimately, I listened.

Well, the "good company" wasn't all that good and went belly up eight years later. The branch manager job that was supposed to take care of me for life disappeared. I then started a souvenir clothing and promotional products company to serve preschools and daycare centers. It was hard work and reasonably profitable until I suffered a fall, head first, down an escalator. Somehow, my body twisted as I was falling and landed on the back of my neck. The resulting back injury made it very difficult to continue operating the business. It was back to the career drawing board. It was at that time, in the mid-2000s, that my wife Diane spotted a story about the New York Voiceover Academy.

It was located in Merrick, New York, which is on Long Island and about a 60-mile commute from our home in Metuchen, New Jersey. It was 2005, and there was no Zoom or FaceTime, and the world still operated on a completely in-person basis. Thus began a series of long commutes from Central New Jersey through New York City and out to Long Island. Each one of those trips proved to be incredibly worthwhile.

The talent instructor at the New York Voiceover Academy was Chuck McKibben, a highly skilled sound engineer and accomplished voice talent. Chuck started out by working at his hometown radio station in Dayton, Ohio, and ended up running the audio operations at Mel Blanc's studio in Hollywood. Mel Blanc, the voice of Bugs Bunny, Barney Rubble, and the oftentimes verbal foil for Jack Benny on both radio and television, remains the superior voice talent in the industry's history. In addition to being a skilled teacher and an incredibly nice guy, Chuck was great to work with and learn from. I dusted off my vocal chops, learned how to add spoken life to the written word, and was back in the saddle. I distinctly remember one night after an especially rewarding session sitting in traffic on the Belt Parkway in Brooklyn; there was a tear in my eye. I felt very torn. I was thankful and happy that I was back doing what I was truly meant to do, but also a bit sad that I had wasted a great deal of time.

I constructed a home studio, which, by 2006 standards, was as good as any commercial recording studio. Small voice jobs began to come in: a regional radio commercial for RE/MAX and nightly recorded telephone forecasts for Weather Phone in New York and Boston, among others. I then decided to try to find some voice jobs outside of my home studio. I ended up working a great job for five seasons as the stadium public address announcer for the Staten Island Yankees, a minor league affiliate of the New York Yankees. Other than my current job hosting *The Weekend* radio show, my gig with the Yankees was the best job I ever had. My responsibilities expanded to working corporate events and hosting dinners at Yankee Stadium. During this time, I was also the fill-in public address announcer for the NHL's New Jersey Devils and, for one quite interesting season, the public address announcer and Assistant General Manager of a professional basketball team. Well, kind of professional at first. It was one of the more interesting and eventful jobs I've ever had.

In the fall of 2006, I saw an ad in *Backstage* magazine that the Brooklyn Wonders were looking for a public address announcer. "What's a Brooklyn Wonder," I wondered. It turns out it was a new team in the American Basketball Association (ABA). Now, this wasn't the ABA known for Julius Erving (Dr. J) back in the '70s; it was a minor league run out of a guy's house in Indiana, with a mish-mosh of teams scattered across the country playing strangely scheduled games in both high school and small college gyms. I was getting back into the voice game, so it seemed like a gig that would garner me some experience and a few extra bucks to add another piece to the puzzle, which was our household budget.

I was hired a few days after sending the team a CD demo (CDs were still quite the rage in '06). The team was owned by a Manhattan financier, hedge fund running, real estate speculation guy. Honestly, I couldn't figure out what the hell he did. After an organizational meeting in an extremely well-appointed twentieth-story office in some gleaming glass tower on Madison Avenue, we prepared for our first home game the following Friday, played at a small college in Brooklyn.

After that first home game, the owner essentially disappeared, didn't return calls, and no one got paid. I was ready to chalk it up as a bad decision and a few wasted weeks, but then I received a phone call. The franchise had just been sold to the family of NBA star Elton Brand. They wanted to give back to the community and provide an opportunity for players who never made it to the NBA to be able to play professionally in New York City so they could remain relevant, showcase their talents, maybe attract the attention of an NBA scout, or more realistically the attention of a professional team overseas.

The Brands changed the name to the Comets, and the team was back up and running. Elton's brother Artie was named the team's General Manager, but Artie lived in Chicago, and this was just prior to smartphones, years before Zoom, and long before today's ubiquitous ability to run anything from anywhere. Thus, he needed help. Artie and I hit it off instantly. He loved how I sounded doing the home games, and out of nowhere asked me to take on the added responsibilities of Assistant General Manager. He offered me a guaranteed salary for the rest of the '06-'07 season to do both the public address during the home games and essentially run the franchise in his absence. I did everything: design the new Comets uniforms, handle relations with the team's home arena, book travel arrangements, keep the head coach happy, and meet Artie for lunch at Newark Airport every two weeks to keep him and the Brand family in the loop.

Things in Comets World then turned quite interesting. A few games were canceled because under-financed teams couldn't afford to travel to Brooklyn to play us. One team that did show up demanded fast food before coming out on the floor to play, which sent me scrambling to the nearest McDonald's to buy 30 Big Macs, 15 orders of fries, and 15 large Cokes. Then something happened I could never have imagined, even with all the craziness surrounding the team.

We had a road game one frigid Saturday evening in February. I rented a large passenger van and drove the team up to Cape Cod to take on the immortal Cape Cod Frenzy. The only reason I went on the trip that weekend was because our radio play-by-play announcer, Lance Medow, was unavailable that night, and I was going to fill in on the broadcast. Our head coach was traveling on his own up to Cape Cod due to a family commitment but promised to be there on time. He wasn't. A few minutes before tip-off, the officials told our players they needed a coach, or the Comets would forfeit the game. The players approached me as I was about to begin the broadcast and told me they needed a coach. We didn't want to forfeit, but our coach was going to be about 45 minutes late. Thus, *please welcome the Interim Head Coach of the Brooklyn Comets: Ed Kalegi.* I coached the first quarter and the first few minutes of the second. Brooklyn defeated Cape Cod 72-67 that night, and, to this day, I claim that victory for myself, making me perhaps the only undefeated head coach in professional basketball history.

We made the ABA playoffs but lost in the first round. The players were a group of incredibly nice guys still pursuing their professional dreams. Alas, at the end of the '06-'07 campaign, Artie flew into Newark and told me over coffee and a Cinnabon in Terminal A that the family would not continue with the team the following season. That meant my career as Brooklyn Comets public address announcer, Assistant General Manager, and Interim Head Coach ended with a handshake, a ridiculously under-cooked pastry, and a two-week severance check. Regardless, it was a good experience.

My next foray into live event work was as a race announcer and entertainment host for the New York Road Runners. For several years, one of my primary duties was to emcee the morning entertainment near the start line of the New York City Marathon. We had a large stage near the Verrazano Bridge, and I had a semi-captive audience of 35,000 people who were all stretching in unison while removing excess layers of clothing. It was a strange sight. The marathon is usually held the first Sunday of November and the first morning of the return to Eastern Standard Time; thus, it's usually dark, damp, and quite chilly. A great perk was that I had access to the large VIP tent backstage, where I could warm up, grab a coffee and a meal, and chat with the politicians and celebrities who were in attendance for the start of the race.

One year, while in the tent, I noticed someone not feeling well; she seemed to have a cold and was using one tiny balled-up tissue. I grabbed a box, which I knew was stored under a table, and brought it over to her. Katie Holmes said thank you and smiled. A little more than a year later, I was working one day as a background actor for the film *The Extra Man*. In the scene, Katie Holmes and Paul Dano chat next to me as we wait for an elevator. The scene continues as Katie and I enter the elevator. She and I would wait inside the elevator as the scene ended, and they would reset the camera and lights for the turnaround shot. As we were in there, I said to her: "I gave you a box of tissues at the marathon last year." She remembered, and we had a nice chat. Three days later, I received a call from the casting director who asked if I wanted six weeks of work on *The Extra Man* as a featured background actor and as the stand-in for John C. Reilly. It was a wonderful experience working very closely with John, Paul, Katie, and Kevin Kline. Thus, today's object lesson is to always be ready to hand out fresh tissue. Good things can happen.

I started doing some non-union background acting in the summer of 2008 to make extra money on days I wasn't doing voiceover or working a game. I was fortunate to spend many days over the next few years working on the sets of many TV shows and films shot in the New York area, including all incarnations of the *Law & Order* franchise: the original *Law & Order*, *Law & Order: SVU*, and *Law & Order: Criminal Intent*. If there had ever been a *Law & Order: Wednesday Night Traffic Court*, I would have been on that one. One day on *SVU*, I nearly hit Christopher Meloni with my car. Fortunately, I had the chance to apologize to Chris years later when he guested on my radio show. Ironically, I got my Screen Actors Guild card not from the background acting but from a vocal role that stemmed from my time with the Yankees.

Sugar is a film detailing the story of a 19-year-old from the Dominican Republic who gets a chance to play professional baseball in the United States. The 2008 baseball drama was casting a vocal role of a stadium public address announcer for a minor league baseball team in Iowa. The producers and directors of the film attended a Staten Island Yankees game to better understand the atmosphere of professional minor league baseball. A few days later, they called the New York Yankees to inquire if I'd be interested in auditioning for the role. Of course, I'd be interested; this was a major motion picture being developed by Sony Pictures Classics.

I received a phone call from the film's casting director, who conferenced me in with the film's directors. They asked if I could send them a vocal sample on a CD because they wanted to cast the role within the next week. I said there was no need to do that and immediately gave them some improvised lines that a baseball stadium announcer would use. The very next thing they heard on that call was: "Fans, join us Saturday, August 4th, when your Staten Island Yankees host the Brooklyn Cyclones. The first 5,000 fans will receive a free beach towel courtesy of Toyota. Game time is 7:30." I then "introduced" a couple of hypothetical players as I would during an actual game to reinforce my sound and style. We had a nice conversation, and the directors thanked me for my time. Later that day, as I was on a train back home after a half day on the *Law and Order* set, my phone rang. The casting director said they decided they didn't need to audition anyone else; the role was mine. One problem, though, she needed my Screen Actors Guild (SAG) identification number. Uh oh. I wasn't in the union. Fortunately, they wanted me badly enough to request a Taft-Hartley exemption, which allowed me to work in the film as long as I joined SAG immediately thereafter. A role in a major film was the easiest way to be allowed into the Screen Actors Guild.

In 2008, entrance into the actor's union was still based on accomplishment and merit, which is why you often hear stories of veteran actors talking about how and when they got their SAG card. It was how you made it, how you got in. This was a big moment for me, and it made me think back to those times when I was on stage in high school. Having my SAG card now also meant double the pay and much more background work, including that six-week gig in *The Extra Man* and the chance to audition for and snag a few small movie roles. Gee, it turns out I would "be in a movie someday." That vocal role in *Sugar* was recorded in a New York City studio, and the session lasted about an hour. I was paid $1,000 for my troubles. Those are good troubles to have, and because of it, I get to sign very tiny residual checks for the rest of my life.

My first taste of hosting a show professionally came in the late summer of 2009 when I was hired for the weekday sports and pop culture show on UBA-TV. UBA was not U-B-A; it was pronounced "ooo-buh" as someone from Staten Island would pronounce the word uber. That's uber as in its original intended definition of "denoting an outstanding or supreme example of a particular kind of person or thing," not the ubiquitous ride-sharing monolith we all tap in our apps today. Anyway, UBA-TV was owned by John Tabacco, a New York financial brokerage owner (from

Staten Island) who dabbled in local conservative politics and seemingly was yearning to become a public figure.

UBA-TV was "internet TV" when streaming video was still trying to figure out what it wanted to be. There was no app, just a very 2009ish website that showed live video and a few archived shows. The facilities, though, were top-notch. The studio was located on Broad Street in Lower Manhattan, only a few buildings away from the New York Stock Exchange. The backdrop, outside the large floor-to-ceiling studio windows, was the hustle and bustle of the Financial District, including Federal agents on patrol with their bomb-sniffing canine companions. In addition to the *Today* show-esque studio, there was a state-of-the-art control room, dressing rooms, make-up rooms, etc. It was a nice place to work.

Tabacco created a morning show that was intended to talk about finance but ended up being whatever he wanted it to be depending on the day, his mood, and the latest supposed outrage being pushed on the front page of the *New York Post*. The 10:00 AM spot belonged to Bob Grant. Grant was a legendary conservative New York City radio talk show host in the '70s, '80s, and '90s who predated Rush Limbaugh and was a more gritty, slightly less polished version. Grant tended to be obnoxious and could be downright racist, sexist, and homophobic on the radio, but by 2009, when he arrived at UBA, Bob was on the 17th hole of his career and had mellowed greatly. The noon slot was hosted by Richard Bey.

Richard worked primarily in Philadelphia and New York but is best known for *The Richard Bey Show*, which began on WWOR-TV in New York in the early '90s and soon was syndicated around the country. It was fun and outrageous. Simply put, Jerry Springer eventually stole Richard's act. Springer's show began as an issues-oriented hour of conversation very similar to what Phil Donahue was already doing quite successfully. Eventually Springer's show morphed into a zany caricature of Richard's. Anyway, Richard is also an extremely gifted talk show host, leans left politically, argues the progressive agenda with great acumen, is always an interesting conversation, and, most importantly, a genuinely nice guy. The 11:00 AM weekday slot was mine. *In the Zone with Ed Kalegi* debuted the day after Labor Day 2009. Nestled between Grant and Bey, it gave me the chance to engage an audience, write, produce, and host a daily TV show in New York City. That ain't too shabby.

UBA-TV was all over the place in terms of programming. Other than Tabacco, Grant, Kalegi, and Bey, the rest of the schedule was a hodgepodge, with the strangest being a guy who would report on the latest New York City mafia news. He took it seriously and had extended interviews with semi-famous family members of New York's most notorious members of organized crime. It was as strange as it sounds. The rap group The Sugar Hill Gang had a weekly talk show where they would also play some of their old music videos, and even Jay-Z dropped by one day to record an episode. Another show was centered around a psychic/medium who took me aside one morning in the makeup room and told me my future was bright and that I would one day write a book. I guess this book. Ooh, spooky, and yes, your hands *are* beginning to sweat.

My ride at UBA didn't last very long. Only two and a half months into my stay there, the entire place shut down. I showed up at 6:30 AM the Monday before Thanksgiving and kept knocking on the door. The street-side studio was dark and eerily empty. It turned out everyone had been notified very late the night before that UBA-TV was no more. Guess who forgot to check his email that morning before commuting from Metuchen to Manhattan? Others who were let go and were in the know speculated that they intended to build "the network" up fast and sell it off just as quickly. The trouble was that there was very little advertising on the website, and talent such as Bob Grant, Richard Bey, and myself were collecting decent paychecks that could no longer be justified with such a shaky business model. In retrospect, it was an idea that was technically ahead of its time, and with the help of a decent app or streaming service such as Roku, it may have worked if it had debuted in 2019 rather than 2009.

With UBA-TV abruptly in the rearview mirror, I immediately dusted off my SAG card and, within a few days, again began doing background work. Yup, back to being the cop looking quite busy at the coffee machine on *Law and Order: SVU.* Trouble is, unless you are working background every single day, which involves commuting in and out of New York City, day and night to locations all over the place and working up to 12 hours at a time, background acting isn't a viable career option, especially for someone married with a hungry six-year-old child and an even hungrier mortgage.

Thus, immediately after the holidays passed, I sent a few of my UBA shows to Mark Chernoff, the longtime program director of WFAN Sports Radio. Chernoff said I was good, but he wasn't looking for anyone at the time. He suggested I reach out to Metro Broadcast Services, which provided twice hourly sports reports for the two New York City news radio stations: WCBS and WINS. I did, but she wasn't looking for sports reporters. Instead, they needed a radio traffic reporter. I had never done a radio traffic report other than a parody of one during a brief stint as a weekend DJ years before at WGPA Radio in Bethlehem, PA. *Here's the latest traffic report: the light in front of the station is red, oops now it's green.* During our initial phone call, Metro's Operations Director asked if I could do the job. I asked for her email address and immediately went into my home studio, recorded a mock New York City traffic report, and sent it to her. Fifteen minutes later, she called back and invited me in for an interview.

Soon after, I began a long stretch as a weekday radio traffic reporter at Metro Traffic, as it was called at the time. It was a bit confusing initially because the sign beside the door read "Shadow Traffic." The company had already been sold and renamed a couple of times and would be again. Located in an office building in the middle of the New Jersey Meadowlands, you would look outside from the ninth-story offices and see MetLife Stadium, countless nondescript warehouses, swamps, more swamps, and even more swamps. It was hard not to contemplate how many of Tony Soprano's "packages" were stashed by Christopher, Paulie, and company in many of those murky, marshy quagmires of convenience.

The studios were dark, quite grimy, and decorated with a purple neon light strip that lined the ceilings in a very strange and almost discomforting way. The overall feel of the Shadow Traffic studios made me recall the overwhelmingly smothering look and feel of the workplace in the Tom Hanks film *Joe Versus the Volcano*: tiny little studios that were poorly lit and rarely, if ever, cleaned.

Inside each studio, a traffic reporter broadcasted repetitive reports on New York City area radio stations. I soon learned that some of those traffic reporters had been in their tiny little studios every weekday since the 1980s. But it was live New York radio, and I embraced it. However, I soon realized the job lacked even the smallest allowance of creativity, and all we were doing was reinforcing the most obvious information. *Delays on the Cross Bronx Expressway, Twenty minutes at the Lincoln Tunnel, Uh oh, there's a broken-down bus in Queens!* It was an exercise of manic redundancy: the same information report after report, day after day after day. You could take a New York radio traffic report recorded five years ago, play it on the air tomorrow afternoon at 4:00, and no one would know the difference. We were telling New York that traffic was slow. Duh.

Certain things, such as frequent time checks and school closings, have disappeared from broadcast radio because they are no longer needed. Radio traffic reports are becoming more irrelevant with each passing day. People have no interest in waiting ten minutes for a traffic report only to hear about roads they aren't traveling. Do you care about a broken-down truck 60 miles from where you are? Today, the best traffic report is simply asking your phone, "Hey Siri, what's the quickest way to Yonkers?"

Despite the monotony, it was a SAG-AFTRA union job that fed my pension, nothing more. It granted no opportunity for imagination, growth, thought, or original expression. The job was the professional equivalent of wheels stuck in the mud, spinning yet going nowhere. *Forty minutes at the Holland Tunnel, thirty minutes at the George Washington Bridge*, yada, yada, and more yada. It truly beat me down at times, and I'm so glad it's in the past.

The general malaise of doing radio traffic reports made me begin to yearn for something better, something bigger. A few years into the job, I began thinking about creating and hosting a radio talk show. I kept thinking back to the brief UBA-TV show, my days doing the radio show back at Rutgers, listening overnight in the '80s to Larry King and Tom Snyder, watching Dick Cavett as a kid back in the '70s, and I asked myself one afternoon while sitting inside my tiny portion of the traffic dungeon: "If not now, then when?"

So, I began recording segments and ideas as a way to get myself back into a more conversational tone rather than the pitter-patter of daily robotic traffic reporting. The aim was to create a strong demo to pitch to radio syndication companies. At first, I recorded samples with a woman who also worked at the traffic job. After several months of recording, listening, and tweaking, we began to shop the show around and generate some interest. Then as an aside, we met with a former radio programmer who was working as an independent consultant.

On a handshake, he agreed to help shop the show, but a week later, the woman I was working with decided instead to try out for a giggly co-host position on a radio show in New York that already had a male talent. It turned out to be a bit of a double-cross as I found out the consultant had pushed her in that direction almost immediately after our handshake. Professional loyalty and commitment are very important to me, and when that happened, I immediately ended my professional relationship with her and my professional relationship with him. She auditioned for that position, and it didn't go particularly well. At last check, she's still toiling in the traffic dungeon. Oh well, karma.

Fast forward about two months to June 2014, and I was driving back to New Jersey from Walt Disney World along with my wife and son. We were somewhere along I-95 in North Carolina when my wife decided she would drive for a while, and I decided to take a nap. Just as I was falling asleep, my phone rang. It was Michael Lichtstein, the Vice President of Programming at Envision Radio Networks. I had a few conversations with Michael a few months prior where we sort of kicked the tires a bit about a show. He said they wanted to make a change with a current weekend show and invited me to visit him at the network's New York office. A few days later, I met with Michael and was offered the chance to take over a three-hour block of *America Weekend.*

At this point, *America Weekend* was a series of three-hour blocks hosted by a few different talk personalities. Stations could take one block, two blocks, or all three. It was explained to me that the network wanted to change things up; they felt both the content and reaction to the shows were lackluster. I listened to what they were currently offering, and lackluster was only the beginning of the problem. The hosts were extremely colloquial. They sounded as if they were from the Midwest, and they only talked about it. It was a nationally syndicated show, but it was all about Chicago and St. Louis. The hosts' presentation was also quite outdated for the mid-twenty-teens: 1970s Top 40 radio voices that relied on stories of little common interest, weird puns, and guest interviews that went nowhere. It wasn't very good. I told Lichtstein I could definitely do better. Was the money great? Absolutely not, but it was a way in through a door that was now wide open.

Thus, on the weekend of July 26, 2014, *America Weekend with Ed Kalegi* debuted on 35 radio stations across the country. I had complete creative control of my own syndicated radio show. I knew in my heart that the best talk radio was conversational talk radio, and that's what I set out to do. I wanted to talk to people that I knew the audience would be interested in hearing from. A few weeks into the show, the network asked if I had any guests on my bucket list that I wanted to book.

There was no list; there was just one name. I wanted Dick Cavett on the show, on my show. I wanted to speak with the person who first lit the fire inside me all those years ago. Two weeks later, I chatted with Dick on the show for about 45 minutes when originally it was supposed to be a ten-minute segment. In the middle of our conversation, he asked: "Do you have to go through your life saying 'Kalegi, spelled the usual way?'" I immediately thought back to being a kid and watching Cavett on my five-inch black and white Sony TV and realized I was extremely fortunate to have this moment and this opportunity. The dream had come true. The conversation with Cavett led to conversations with Dick Van Dyke, Carol Burnett, Julie Andrews, and on and on and on.

The show has grown and evolved over time into what is heard now on *The Weekend with Ed Kalegi.* One-on-one conversations have become the nucleus of what I do. Over the years, I dabbled a couple of times with having a co-host, but it changed the timbre and flow of the program. A one-on-one chat with an interesting author, celebrity, newsmaker, or expert makes for the perfect temporary co-host and creates quality conversation, which is the best listen of all.

Whether my guests are famous or not, I do think it's important to recognize the impact of their work, especially if that work has touched so many lives. I also believe it's interesting to learn about the person behind the creative work. Over the years, I've had the pleasure of speaking with hundreds of guests, and quite honestly, I'm just getting started as there are so many more folks to speak with.

Not very long ago, I began to think that many of the conversations I've had until this point could be the framework of a book. Well, this is that book. What follows is a collection of many of my favorite conversations which have aired on my show. It was quite a ride to go back, write about them, and realize just how many folks whose work I've enjoyed have appeared on the program. I'm very grateful for the opportunities I've had and appreciate that I finally pursued what I was meant to do. Whatever *your* dream is, whatever *you* want to do, go after it. *Never* stop trying and remember the saddest question you can be left asking yourself is "What if?"

Turn your "what if" into a "what is."

I hope you enjoy these conversations as much as I did. Here we go.

It was great to say hello to...

1

Carol Burnett

Television Personality, Comedian, and Entertainer

I'm getting fan mail from nine-year-olds!

***

Television in 1978 looked nothing like it did in 1967. There was a seismic change in what we watched in primetime, but there was one constant during that period: *The Carol Burnett Show* on CBS. Carol Burnett is the woman who practically owned television during this period and did so by giving America its greatest variety show. Variety shows were pretty common fare at the time, and many were quite forgettable, but *The Carol Burnett Show* was different. It was a consistently funny, always innovative combination of comedy and music. It set a high bar every week and always reached it. Carol surrounded herself with a brilliant ensemble cast: Harvey Korman, Tim Conway, Vicki Lawrence, along with Lyle Waggoner in the early years, and even Dick Van Dyke for part of one season. That cast created a stable of memorable characters that became a part of the fiber and fabric of 1970s American pop culture. Many of the sketches featuring Conway and Korman remain some of the funniest in television history.

It was also a place where iconic guest stars would stop by as the show displayed great respect for the entire entertainment industry. It could be argued that during the '70s, *The Carol Burnett Show* was the center of that industry. Just hearing her voice as we spoke brought back the feeling of being stretched out on the shag carpet in front of the floor-model color TV smack dab in the middle of a weekend back in 1970-something.

It was great to say hello to Carol Burnett.

As I waited for her to come on the line to chat about her book *In Such Good Company,* I started thinking of the perfect word to describe Carol as I introduced her to my listeners. Here's someone who has received the Presidential Medal of Freedom, the Mark Twain Prize for American Humor, and is a Kennedy Center honoree. One word quickly came to mind. Icon.

"She is an icon. She is Carol Burnett. Carol, welcome to the show."

Thank you, Ed. How are you today?

I told Carol I was absolutely terrific, especially since I was speaking with her. I chose to begin our time together by asking how her legendary CBS show came to be in the first place. The mid-1960s wasn't a time when many women were headlining their own variety shows. I was very surprised by what Carol said when I asked what CBS said when she first pitched them the idea for the show.

Actually, Ed, I didn't pitch it. What happened was when I was on The Garry Moore Show, *CBS came to me and wanted to put me under a ten-year contract. I said great, which would mean they would pay me a decent amount of money every year to do one special and maybe two guest shots on their sitcoms. But there was a caveat in the first five years because Ed, I had some kind of a swell agent. He said: 'If Carol wants to do a one-hour variety show, all she would have to do is push the button, and CBS would have to put it on for 31 one-hour shows.' I thought, oh, I'll never want to, I don't think I could host a show. I didn't think that I would ever want to do that. Well, the five years were almost up, and my husband and I looked at each other. We said, you know what? Let's push that button.*

Talk about a smart agent. He literally took a contract that was designed primarily to keep Carol in-house for a decade, and thus away from the other networks, and turned it into a bridge that allowed Carol to become one of the biggest stars the network has ever had. It proves that good agents are worth every dime, but great agents are worth every dollar. It does make one wonder if network lawyers ever really read all the contingencies buried deep within Paragraph this and Section that. Carol told me she believes no one ever had a contract clause like it before, and certainly not since. I asked what happened when she actually went ahead and pushed that button.

I reached out to CBS the last week of '66. I called New York and talked to one of the vice presidents, and I said: 'Hi, I'm gonna push that button.' They had totally forgotten. What button? I said: 'You know where I get to do 31?' Well, I think they got a lot of lawyers out of Christmas parties that night. He called back the next day and he said: 'Yeah, I see that in the contract but, look Carol, variety is a man's game. It's Sid Caesar, it's Milton Berle, it's Jackie Gleason. Now it's Dean Martin. We've got this great sitcom we'd love you to do. It's a half hour show called Here's Agnes.*' I told him I didn't want to be Agnes every week. I wanted to be different characters, that's what I learned to do on The Garry Moore Show and have music and guest stars and a rep company and so forth. So, they had to put us on the air, but they really had no faith in us.*

Wow, they actually tried to weasel out of the deal! I love the choice of male talents the CBS executive quoted to Carol to explain why she didn't belong. Remember, as Carol told me, this was the very end of 1966. At that time, Caesar, Berle, and Gleason were not the hippest or most contemporary of entertainers. All three are more associated with the 1950s rather than the 1960s. True, Dean Martin was new-ish to the variety show game in the late '60s, but his personality, crooning, and constant tuxedo were hallmarks of a Vegas ballroom in '58. That CBS executive was seemingly rooted in looking at television's past rather than the possibilities of its future, and considering the way the industry operated at the time, perhaps he had an issue with a woman headlining a variety show. CBS had to give in because a contract is a contract, but isn't it deliciously ironic that even though they tried to squirm out of the agreement, the powers that be at the network ended up looking like geniuses for the next eleven years? Folks, irony can become the world's greatest concealer for stupidity, even better than anything Max Factor could ever apply.

Carol was a bit more diplomatic: *"I have to give them credit because after we were on for about three or four weeks and were doing well, they called and said, 'you were right, and we're very happy that you're doing this.' And they supported us for all that time, all eleven years."*

In order to illustrate my perspective of *The Carol Burnett Show,* I explained that the show ran on CBS when I was between the ages of zero and eleven, so I started when the show did, literally. As a quick aside, when I made that "age of zero" comment during our conversation, Carol laughed. I made Carol Burnett laugh! How cool is that? Anyway, back to the book. I told Carol that what I believe always made her show special, be it watching it back then and even today on DVD, YouTube, or the classic TV channels, is that kids can watch with their parents and their grandparents, and everyone laughs together.

Yes!

"Everyone gets it," I continued. "There's nothing wrong with big belly laughs, especially when families can laugh together."

I agree, and when we were on, that Saturday night lineup was amazing because it was All in the Family, M*A*S*H, The Mary Tyler Moore Show, The Bob Newhart Show, *and us. And it was before you could record anything, so it was really appointment television. I'm thrilled today that because of Time-Life issuing the DVDs of the full show and the fact that I have a YouTube channel, we're showing some of the best sketches. I'm getting fan mail from nine-year-olds!*

"That's incredible, Carol."

Oh Ed, and from teenagers and people in their twenties and everything. Somebody asked how I explain that. My answer is funny, is funny. I dare anybody to watch Tim and Harvey in the dentist sketch. It should go in the time capsule because it's just one of the funniest things and it holds up, and it's over 50 years since they did it.

The listeners didn't realize it, but Carol inadvertently proved clairvoyant as she went exactly where I planned to go next: the infamous sketch where Tim Conway plays the bumbling dentist and Harvey Korman is the patient. It is a masterclass in television comedy as Conway keeps giving himself injections of Novocain by accident. I told Carol about how that previous weekend, as I was preparing for our conversation, my son came into the room and discovered me watching the dentist sketch. He sat down, watched it for the first time, and laughed as hard as I'd ever seen him laugh.

"Carol," I said, "Your show is timeless as it goes from generation to generation."

That's right, and I think it's a blessing. We didn't really start out thinking that it would be the little Energizer bunny that it's become. We didn't make it timely. In other words, we didn't say, okay, what happened this week in the news? So, everything holds up pretty well. I mean, we sometimes did something that, you know, was current, but most of the time, it was all about just being funny for funny sake as opposed to being edgy or totally satirical.

This is when I got up on my proverbial soapbox. I reiterated to Carol how there's never anything wrong with a good and hearty belly laugh, but nowadays, it seems as if many times that laugh is accompanied by and must be absorbed with an abrasive edge and that the humor itself is almost forcibly topical.

I couldn't agree more. I'm not a prude by any stretch of the imagination, but I find that some of it is so edgy, and they just want to be blue. If it's just being blue for blue's sake and just to say, 'oh, aren't we just so clever?' I guess what I miss is cleverness.

"Carol, it's a bit lazy too." Again, she agreed and cited *All in the Family* as an example of brilliant writing. She then added *The Mary*

Tyler Moore Show and *The Dick Van Dyke Show* as examples of shows she considers brilliantly written without stooping to be edgy.

I then pivoted to the tremendous number of guest stars who appeared on the Burnett show. Many times, they were superstars. Carol isn't only someone *in* show business, she *loves* show business, and her choices of guest stars simply reinforced that love. I had to know if there was a certain special one.

"As you look back, who was your, 'Oh my God, I actually got to work with...' person, who was that for you?"

There is more than one: Bing Crosby, Rita Hayworth. I mean, these are all names that your son wouldn't know, but I grew up going to the movies and seeing these icons.

"They were your inspiration," I replied, "and now you're working with them."

Sure. these movie stars: Lana Turner, Betty Grabel, even Gloria Swanson, were the people that just blew me away, and to be able to sing with Ella Fitzgerald, with Ray Charles. I can go on and on and on. It was just such a thrill for me because I was a real movie nut when I was a kid growing up. So, to have these people come on my show and get in the sandbox with me, yeah, it was absolutely thrilling.

I could understand exactly what she was saying because here I was on my show, speaking with someone I watched almost religiously when I was a kid. Remember when I mentioned stretching out on that shag carpet in front of the TV to watch her show? As I look back, it was more than just watching a TV show; it was part of a comfortable ritual wedged deep within those 500-some-odd weekends of a pre-teenage childhood. *The Carol Burnett Show* was an important part of the soundtrack of that childhood. My childhood. Remember also when I mentioned I was searching for the best word to describe Carol when our conversation began? At this moment, near the end of our time together, the perfect way to conclude things with Carol then came to me.

"Now when people ask me my oh my God moment," I said, "I can tell them it's the day I had Carol Burnett on *my* show."

Wow, thank you, Ed, said Carol quite graciously.

It turns out that Saturday nights, thick shag carpet, and floor model color televisions never really go out of style. They simply live in our minds forever.

2

Dick Van Dyke

Actor, Entertainer, and Comedian

Being youthful and beautiful and a rockstar is very important.

***

It must be wonderful to be someone whose mere mention of their name elicits a smile. There are very few entertainers who have not only transcended decades of time but maintained a place in the hearts and minds of generations of people. Dick Van Dyke is a member of that very select club.

Dick's body of work is so vast we can each view his career through our own prism. For as many that remember him best as comedy writer Rob Petrie on *The Dick Van Dyke Show*, there are probably as many younger television viewers who remember Dick as Dr. Mark Sloan on *Diagnosis Murder*. I'm the oddball in the group. My first remembrance of Dick was in the role of Caractacus Potts in the 1968 film *Chitty Chitty Bang Bang*. Growing up, CBS showed the film annually during the '70s, and watching the film each year, at least for me, represented the passing of another milepost as I journeyed through childhood. And, of course, we all remember Dick as Burt in *Mary Poppins*, a role in which Walt Disney personally cast him.

In recent years, as Dick has progressed through his nineties, he has not only maintained relevance, but he also represents a wonderful example of aging without reservation, without fear, and with an almost childlike wonder to experience life every day at its fullest. He personifies inspiration. One of the fringe benefits of hosting a show like mine is getting the chance every once in a while to talk with an icon.

It was great to say hello to Dick Van Dyke.

The first thing I noticed when Dick came on the line as he was in Los Angeles and I was in New Jersey was his voice. His voice has always been his calling card: deep, resonant, somewhat unique, and mysteriously soothing. It felt as if I was about to chat with an old friend, albeit a friend I'd never actually met, until now. I welcomed him to the show by telling the audience the obvious: that he has been a part of the fiber and fabric of American pop culture for 60 years.

Thank you, Ed, said Dick in that unmistakable Van Dyke voice.

I didn't want to begin the conversation as a retrospective, but as one with contemporary relevance. I started by mentioning that Dick had recently talked about something he calls the Gray Rights Movement, which is a revolution to change the way we think about aging. Obviously, most would agree that Dick is the perfect person to spearhead such a conversation.

They apparently noticed I'm a little spryer than my contemporaries, especially the dead ones, joked Dick. *I realized how much more there is to say about aging including attitude, open mindedness, a certain spirituality, and of course health. The key, though, is to keep moving.*

I immediately thought of something I read years before. Back in the late '60s on the set of *Chitty Chitty Bang Bang,* Dick pulled a muscle and went to see the doctor. Not thinking it was anything more than something which would call for a few days of rest, Dick was quite surprised when the doctor told him it was the onset of arthritis and even mentioned the possibility of ending up in a wheelchair in only a few short years.

Yeah Ed, that really threw a scare into me because I didn't want to give up dancing or anything else and so I've kept moving every day and I do have arthritis and it has aged along with me, but it really doesn't bother me. I stretch every day. I go to the gym every day and I'm trying to convince people to not throw in the towel. You know, the concept of aging in this country is just horrific. Young people would rather die before they get old. Being youthful and beautiful and a rockstar is very important, but there's so much you can do to maintain that as you grow older.

After I somehow was able to get Dick Van Dyke to use the word rockstar in a sentence, I decided it was a good time to pivot to his legendary career. I began with the 60-year friendship he shared with Carl Reiner, who passed away in 2020 at the age of 98. If there was no Carl Reiner, there never would have been *The Dick Van Dyke Show.* Dick reminded our listeners that Carl had done the pilot with Carl, himself, playing the lead role. The network liked the script but told Reiner to *get a better actor for your part.* Carl then thought of Dick, who he had seen on Broadway and brought Dick out to Hollywood to reshoot the pilot. It can be said that things worked out.

The Dick Van Dyke Show was perhaps the first American sitcom that seemed real. You believed these characters could really exist and exist within the situation presented. Rob Petrie was a guy who worked in New York City and dealt with relatable problems at work, then took the train back up to New Rochelle where he dealt with relatable problems at home. It was done with a refreshing comedic sophistication. Television audiences were used to seeing Lucy Ricardo flailing her legs while trapped head first in a working washing machine and Ralph Kramden waving his arms and screaming to the high heavens because he had just closed a drawer on his hand. *The Dick Van Dyke Show* was different. These were fleshed out comedic characters, not overly exaggerated. There's a big difference between the two. It brought smart humor and a much-needed sophistication to TV.

Who cared if eleven-year-olds didn't get it or didn't want to watch it? Primetime television still hadn't fully matured yet, and that wouldn't happen for almost another decade, but *The Dick Van Dyke Show* was the beginning of its adolescence.

Ed, we had five unbelievable years, and it was both creative and fun. Morey Amsterdam said it was like going to a party every day. Carl was one of the wisest human beings I've ever known. He was my favorite person in the world.

Dick and Carl also collaborated on the film *The Comic,* a poignant look into the life of a former silent film star who is struggling to maintain professional relevance and personal purpose at the end of the 1960s.

"Dick, *The Comic* is a brilliant movie, which was also written by Carl Reiner if I remember correctly."

You're right. You know, we found that script on the shelf at Columbia. Really, it had just been laying around. So, Aaron Ruben, Carl, and I sat down, and we rewrote it and actually kinda rewrote it every day. But not many people saw that movie. I felt it was authentic about that time of the film industry. It caught a certain flavor that I liked.

Dick was correct when he stated that not many people saw *The Comic,* at least at the time it was released. It debuted in 1969 and younger audiences perhaps had little interest in a film which rooted itself in the troubles of a performer whose heyday was in the days of Buster Keaton, Stan Laurel, and Harold Lloyd, even though the film touched on themes very pertinent in 1969. Fortunately, the film eventually found a certain level of both acclaim and appreciation for both its intent and its presentation. I believe it was a matter of the right film at the wrong time. America was still only a few years removed from *The Dick Van Dyke Show* and *Mary Poppins,* it wasn't yet ready for this side of Van Dyke.

I've always been struck by Van Dyke's versatility. I firmly believe he gets short-changed when it comes to his dramatic abilities, Exhibit One being his eight seasons playing Dr. Mark Sloan on the CBS series *Diagnosis Murder*. Another is a guest spot on one of my favorite *Columbo* episodes where Dick played the scheming and murderous photographer Paul Galesko in "Negative Reaction." Perhaps, Dick's greatest dramatic achievement was as an alcoholic public relations executive in the rarely seen 1974 film *The Morning After*. What makes Dick's performance in this role even more intriguing is the well-known fact that Dick, himself, endured his own battles with alcohol not very long before the film was shot. I asked Dick if it was difficult for him to switch from comedy to drama and from drama back to comedy.

Well, you know, most serious actors say that comedy is the hardest, but for me, it's the other way around. Comedy and music have a rhythm that I can feel but drama has a whole different beat, and I have trouble with it.

I was a bit shocked when Dick admitted he has trouble with drama, but he then quickly jumped into a comment about *The Morning After*.

I was quite proud of The Morning After. *I find that it's used in a lot of rehab centers. I've talked to people who've come out of rehab and were impressed and helped by the movie, so it's doing some good.*

Dick first achieved national notoriety on the Broadway stage, winning the 1961 Tony Award for Best Featured Actor in a Musical. The role which turned Dick Van Dyke into a star was that of struggling songwriter Alburt Peterson in *Bye Bye Birdie*. Starring alongside Chita Rivera and Paul Lynde, the world discovered that Dick was a leading man who could act, sing, and dance. Dick was the complete package and *Birdie* was the perfect vehicle for Van Dyke. Interesting though, I did stumble across a juicy little nugget while doing some research for our conversation.

"Dick, I was surprised to learn just yesterday that you auditioned for a lesser role in *Birdie*. Gower Champion saw your audition and then told you he wanted you to play Albert. That must've been quite a surprise."

Oh God, it was. I went in and auditioned and sang a little tune, I think from The Music Man, *and did my semblance of a kind of a soft-shoe.*

Gower came up on the stage and said "You're Albert, you've got the part." I told him I don't dance and he said not to worry they would teach me, and my God, did he ever. I discovered dance.

Champion, who himself won two Tony Awards for *Birdie* for direction and choreography, not only introduced Dick to dance but, as Dick himself admits, changed his career with one song.

What changed my career was when we were in Philadelphia doing previews. The guys overnight wrote a song called "Put on a Happy Face" for Chita Rivera. They brought it down to the set and everybody loved it and Gower Champion said "look, the skinny kid hasn't got anything doing the first act, let him have the song." And that pretty well changed my life.

I've written earlier about my time in the drama department at Bishop George Ahr/St. Thomas Aquinas High School in Edison, NJ, and how it shaped me as a performer. The highlight of that time for me was our production of *Bye Bye Birdie.* It was during my junior year and I played the role of Harry McAfee, who was played so incredibly well by Paul Lynde both on the Broadway stage and in the 1963 film. A few weeks before our show opened, our director Gordon Inverno, Jr gathered the company in our school's theater and had us watch the film version of *Birdie.* It was hard for me not to think back to that time as Dick and I chatted about *Birdie.* At this point of our conversation, I could no longer resist, I had to mention it.

"Dick, people my age, everyone who did high school musical theater back in the 1980s did *Bye Bye Birdie,* as we did at my school, it was a rite of passage."

Ed, I think I've seen them all, said Dick with a hearty laugh.

"Yeah, but ours was the best," I replied with a proud wink in my voice.

At this point, as my time with Dick was coming to a close, I searched my mind for the one question which would tie the perfect bow around our conversation. I found it.

"Dick, what is the most surprising thing you've discovered as you have grown older?"

Oh, it is full of surprises! I remember when I turned 80, I said, well this is satisfactory. I didn't realize though it would be a little downhill from that. But what surprises me is, despite having arthritis most of my life, I'm still very, very active. I've got a lot of spring in my step, I still dance and sing, and I haven't really slowed down. I don't play tennis anymore and I don't run the 100-yard dash anymore. But you have to replace it. And, yes, you lose contemporaries. So, you need to get some young friends. You have to stay social. It's so important. And keep the brain going.

Dick had just offered some of the most important advice ever heard on my show, and to use a phrase better recognized by Dick's newer and younger friends, not only does Dick Van Dyke talk the talk, he walks the walk. Dick added that it's also important to sing and dance, even if you stink at it. Sing and dance anyway. It was a pitch perfect ending to a wonderful conversation.

"Dick, this has been a dream come true, thanks for joining me."

It's been a pleasure for me, thank you, Ed.

I drove home from the studio that evening and as I went into my office, I saw something on the shelf above the TV that I hadn't truly noticed in quite a long time: my 1984 "Gordy" Award for Outstanding Performance by an Actor in *Bye Bye Birdie*. I reached for it, blew the light coating of dust off of it, and smiled.

How could I not? In some strange and now quite wonderful way, it had all come full circle.

3

Cindy Williams

Actor, Producer, and Writer

The writers had left a copy of the* Wall Street Journal *on the table. Penny and I read the headline: "Laverne & Shirley Send ABC Stocks Through the Roof."

***

Over the many years that I've hosted the show, I've had conversations with hundreds of people. Many of these encounters remain quite memorable, for a variety of reasons. But there is one that truly sticks out, mainly because of her kind and very generous demeanor that easily bridged a 3,000-mile phone connection. Hers was a humble and sweet personality, even though at one time she was one of the biggest stars on television. I fondly remember our wonderful conversation.

It was great to say hello to Cindy Williams.

I had the pleasure to talk with Cindy around the time of the publication of her memoir: *Shirley, I Jest! A Storied Life*. Our time together was arranged by a mutual friend, literary agent Diane Nine who is based in Washington, DC. As an aside, Diane has provided me with a myriad of wonderful guests over the years and being able to have Cindy on my show was phenomenal.

I knew this conversation would be different the moment the studio phone rang, Cindy was truly thankful and appreciative to be on the show. We chatted for a moment or two and then it was time to record. Off we went.

"My next guest is one of the iconic television stars of the late '70s and early '80s. On January 27th, 1976, *Laverne & Shirley* debuted on ABC in front of an audience of 36 million viewers making it the number one show on television. She's also known for playing Lori Henderson in the groundbreaking film *American Graffiti* and she just released a terrific book: *Shirley, I Jest! A Storied Life*. It is quite a pleasure to say hello to Cindy Williams. Cindy, welcome to the show."

Thank you, Ed. Thank you for having me.

I always try to convey to a guest, especially an actor or entertainer who was a part of a long running TV series many years ago, how old I was during the series' initial run. This way, they can better understand my perspective on the show.

"Cindy, I was nine years old when *Laverne & Shirley* first hit the air and every Tuesday night at 8:30 I was in front of my TV watching you."

And I was only 12, myself, replied Cindy, which brought a big laugh out of me. *Ed, that's quite a compliment, thank you so much.*

I then told Cindy how much I enjoyed her book, which I read over the few nights just prior to our conversation. The book is so much more than just *Laverne & Shirley*, it's Cindy's very introspective look at both her life and her career. I asked her why she decided to write it.

Some years ago, my collaborator asked me if I was interested in doing a book. I said that I wasn't interested in writing a tell-all, I was only interested in writing something that is fun, with antidotes, fun stories, something upbeat. Dave Smitherman agreed with that. But it's very tough to sell that idea because publishers don't like anything positive. It's like if you said, "Oh,

I wanna do a news show, but only happy news, just the happy news that's going on in the world." People would laugh you out of the room. And so, it took 12 years to finally get publishers to say alright, we'll do that book. But they also said we'd also like a little bit about your childhood, your early years, and stuff like that. I was gonna try and steer away from that because I didn't have the greatest childhood in the world and I didn't want it to be a downer. But I found a way to do it where it was just interesting and not a downer.

In the book, Cindy talks about her family life in a very revealing and extremely tasteful way. She talks about her mom and dad, including her father's drinking issue, but she does it in a way which is quite uplifting and discusses a childhood which is probably very reminiscent of many other childhoods, be it back when Cindy was growing up and even today. I wondered if Cindy was surprised by how honest and open she is in the book.

I tried to stay loyal to being honest, and to being the child of an alcoholic. But I did try to pick out things about my childhood that were interesting and about my father's drinking. There's nothing interesting about being six years old and having your dad leave you in the cab of his truck when he goes into a bar drinking. But it's certainly got a compelling aspect to it and when you see the picture of it, I survived it and I survived it well. I don't say there aren't shadows that follow me around, even to this day, as you can never shake them if you're the child of an alcoholic.

Cindy's open and honest discussion about her family life and her early years set the stage for the success that her career eventually became. But the soundstages of Hollywood were not her initial intended destination. Cindy wanted to be an ER nurse, but she couldn't stand the sight of blood.

That was one of the problems, said Cindy with a chuckle. *Yes, that was a major problem. Plus the needles and also I felt too sorry for the little frog when they, you know, anesthetized him and then dissected it. I just couldn't bear the thought of that. But I also could not pass biology in high school with higher than a C minus average. I had to take it twice in summer school and I did learn some things, but I learned enough to know that I would not become a nurse.*

So, with that dissected frog firmly in Cindy's rearview mirror, it was on to Los Angeles City College and the pursuit of an acting career. Cindy had some early appearances on shows such as *Room 222* and *Nanny and the Professor*, but it was her role as Laurie Henderson in the groundbreaking film *American Graffiti*, which truly launched her career.

"Cindy, *American Graffiti* was made on a shoestring budget of $700,000 by some young filmmaker named George Lucas. Gee, I wonder whatever became of him?"

Hmm, yeah, where is he? replied Cindy with an obvious wink in her voice.

"That film had to be quite an experience for you."

It was, it was for everyone. We just thought we were doing a hot rod movie until two weeks into it when George had us come and watch an assemblage of what he had put together, about 20 minutes with music. And when we all saw it, we knew we were in something that was otherworldly. Ed, it was something very special. But, while we were shooting it, we just thought we were doing a kind of a high school soap opera, hot rod movie. And it was all shot in only 28 nights.

"Twenty-eight nights and one morning," I emphasized. "That one morning includes shooting one of the most important scenes of the film. That's the drag race towards the end of the film, between Paul Le Mat's character and Harrison Ford's character. Cindy, this is something I promised myself that if I ever had the chance to talk to you, I would ask you about. You're in the car with Harrison and we see the '55 Chevy veer off the road. Then it rolls over three times. Then it catches fire. You get out of the car and through the pure magic of the movies, you merely have a smudge on your cheek, a couple of hairs out of place, and a slight pull of the letterman sweater. It's amazing how those things happen, is it not?"

Isn't it though?

Cindy told me that scene was shot during a very frenetic day on set. They had only about twenty minutes to shoot what is a very pivotal part of the film. It was left to almost the last day of shooting and Cindy and Ron Howard, who played Cindy's on-again, off-again, and eventually on-again boyfriend in the film, had already been released for the day. They were out of costume when the first assistant director told them that Lucas wanted to shoot the end scene immediately. So, back the both of them went into costume and makeup and they ran back out onto the set, which was the roadside aftermath of the car crash caused by the drag race.

Cindy said that scene where she's screaming at and hitting an injured Harrison Ford as he's pulled away from his wrecked car was a near total improvisation because of the time constraints, but it worked extremely well and it became one of Cindy's favorite scenes in the film.

Soon after *American Graffiti*, Cindy appeared in a very underrated film of the time: 1974's *The Conversation*, which starred Gene Hackman and was directed by Francis Ford Coppola. Pretty soon thereafter, Cindy was writing for another Coppola project along with Penny Marshall, when along came a chance to guest star on the mega hit sitcom, *Happy Days*. It changed her career and her life forever.

Yep, I guess you could say that.

I asked Cindy to fill in the blanks and flesh out exactly what happened.

Penny and I were one of the teams of writers who were writing a bicentennial spoof that Francis Coppola was producing called My Country Tis of Thee. *One day Penny's brother, Garry, called and said, "Look, I have these two characters on Happy Days that I want you and Cindy to come and play. They're called Laverne and Shirley, and they're two girls who date the fleet." That's how he explained them and asked if we would take a week off and come over and do it. I needed the money, so we took a week off and went over and did it.*

Cindy then surprised me a bit when she told me that when Garry called, she still had not seen a single episode of *Happy Days*. She mentioned that her sister was an extra on the show and she had told Cindy how great both Henry Winkler and Ron Howard were. Now, any astute watcher of *Happy Days* back in the day would agree that the characters of Laverne DeFazio and Shirley Feeney were much different when they first showed up in the episode where Fonzie sets up a double date for himself and Richie with Laverne and Shirley. Actually, much different might be an understatement. Cindy's original interpretation of the Shirley character was worlds away from what would become the Shirley Feeney that America would fall in love with and welcome into their homes for the rest of the decade.

During the first rehearsal of that Happy Days *episode, we played them as total down and out floozies. I mean, we came on the soundstage smoking cigarettes and flicked them across the room when we spotted Richie and Fonzie. That's when Jerry Paris, who was directing it, screamed, "Stop! Penny, Cindy, what do you think you're doing? You can't smoke cigarettes! This is Family Hour!" We had no idea what he was talking about. Jerry told us to enter again and this time we just chewed gum.*

Other than Laverne and Shirley coming off as, well, let's just say less than Girl Scouts in that *Happy Days* episode, the other noticeable difference was Cindy's accent. She gave Shirley a very thick Brooklyn accent, almost as distinctive as Penny Marshall's innate Bronx accent. Yes, folks, there is a definite difference between the two accents even though the two boroughs are separated by only a long subway ride. That Brooklyn accent, which sounded quite authentic even for a girl from Van Nuys, California, even lasted into the first few episodes of *Laverne & Shirley*, when it faded away and Shirley Feeney from then on sounded very non-colloquial.

The *Happy Days* episode was shot and Penny and Cindy went back to their writing jobs with Coppola. Three weeks later, the phone rang. It was the type of phone call any actor dreams of receiving.

Someone from Garry's office called and said they wanted to spin our two characters off. We needed to have it explained to us what that meant, what a spinoff was really, and they said your own show. It ended up that ABC bought four shows to put on the air, and Penny and I each thought, you know, that'd be that.

Well, that wasn't that. Thirty-six million people watched the first episode of *Laverne & Shirley* when it debuted in the slot immediately following *Happy Days* on January 27, 1976. True, *Laverne & Shirley* benefited from *Happy Days,* which at that point was a true national pop culture phenomenon. In the mid-1970s, there was a very interesting nostalgic yearning for the 1950s. The early '70s Broadway musical *Grease,* which was turned into a blockbuster film in 1978, led the theoretical charge back into time and was joined by both *Happy Days* and *Laverne & Shirley*. The mid to late 1970s in America were a time, first of political scandal, and then one of difficult domestic circumstances. *Laverne & Shirley* was a sitcom with contemporary sensitivities and humor set in a time, twenty years earlier, which was perceived to be one of greater happiness and innocence. It came around at the perfect time. America needed Laverne DeFazio and Shirley Feeney.

"Cindy, how long did it take before you realized and before Penny realized, just how really big this show was becoming?"

We had no clue. I remember Garry coming down and saying, "Look at our numbers! Look at what the Nielsen ratings are for the show." Penny and I looked and it was like 36 million. We had no concept, and when I tell you none, I mean none. In my mind, I wasn't thinking that's the number of people watching me and Penny and the cast, you know? I was just thinking, wow, that's a lot of people in America. Then one day Penny and I were alone on the set. The writers had left a copy of the Wall Street Journal *on the table. Penny and I read the headline: 'Laverne & Shirley Send ABC Stocks Through the Roof.' I said to Penny, "That's you and me. What do you think that means?" Penny said, "It must be good."*

Cindy Williams and Penny Marshall were now both household names and household faces. Later in 1976, they were invited to be in the Macy's Thanksgiving Day Parade in New York City. Cindy told me parade watchers literally jumped the barriers and started running towards the float upon which Cindy and Penny were riding. The police needed to move in and stop them. This was now approaching Beatles level.

Ed, that's when these distant bells went off that we were popular, we were the popular girls on campus.

That popularity continued for many years but then, as often happens, leave it to the executives to begin to ruin a good thing. While *Happy Days* literally had its jump the shark moment, some may argue *Laverne & Shirley* had its moment when the decision was made to move the setting of the show from Milwaukee to Hollywood. I asked Cindy why they decided to pull them out of that basement apartment, out of the Shotz brewery and the Pizza Bowl, and move Laverne and Shirley out to California.

You know, Ed, Penny and I argued and argued until we were blue in the face with Garry about that, but he was hellbent to move them to Hollywood. He said, "You'll have more fun. We can bring more guest stars in." We said, "No, it'll take the whole flavor out of the show." I remember we were in Penny's kitchen arguing with him and he showed us the scheme of the set and we did not like it. Nobody did, none of the cast liked it. But that's what Garry wanted to do and you're not gonna argue with genius like that, at least not for too long.

I then brought up season eight, at this point, Cindy was married to Bill Hudson and she was four months pregnant. When production for the season began, Cindy found out they planned on shooting on her due date. Things soon became very interesting for Cindy.

Things got a little hairy there. I thought there was a mistake, and this was in the beginning before lawyers got involved, I said, you know, you've got me working on my due date, so I need to change this around. And they said, no, we've already done the schedule for the season. And that's it. Now mind you, I was the first person that I can think of who had come back to a show, especially on the Paramount lot, and was pregnant. I don't think peo-

ple knew quite what to do with a pregnant woman. You know, I was sad to leave, but I just couldn't make it work. Nobody could at that point.

Cindy and Paramount eventually settled their differences out of court and Cindy was released from her contract. The final season of the show continued after Cindy had appeared in the first two episodes with Penny Marshall essentially doing a solo. ABC then removed the show from its schedule at the end of the 1982-83 season. It is a stark reminder of how the early '80s were a much different time in terms of women's rights, employee rights, and corporate sensitivities especially for someone who helped make her employer millions of dollars during a six-and-a-half-year period. So much for the good old days, right?

Even though best remembered as Shirley Feeney, Cindy continued to appear on TV quite regularly through the years including as a series regular in *Sami*, a ten-episode series which dropped on Amazon Prime in January of 2023.

My conversation with Cindy, at least for the show, was now coming to an end. I thanked her on the air for being such a wonderful guest and we said our official on-air goodbyes. The board-op at the radio station ended the recording and I took a long, finishing gulp from my now lukewarm Dunkin' Donuts coffee cup. The phone line was still open and Cindy and I then had an after-interview chat which lasted close to twenty minutes. We talked a little deeper about some of the things we had discussed on the air and she expressed a true and heartfelt gratitude for me having her on my show. It was perhaps the sincerest thank you I have ever received from a guest. I told Cindy, how could I not have her on the show? I explained to her how much prime time television I consumed way back when and that she was a very vivid part of my childhood and early teenage years. I hope she knew how much it meant for me to have a conversation with her.

I vividly remember then saying goodbye to Cindy and finishing with the phrase, "Until next time."

My conversation with Cindy stayed with me for quite a long time and I always intended to have her back on the show. Every year, I travel to Los Angeles to visit with publicists and record a few in-person conversations. In late 2022, as I began to think about 2023, I thought a follow up conversation with Cindy, this time chatting together in the same place, would be terrific. But unfortunately, I waited too long. I was sitting in the studio one afternoon in late January of 2023 and glanced up at the TV, which was muted. The graphic at the bottom of the screen read: "Laverne & Shirley Star Cindy Williams Dies."

I truly felt profoundly sad. An extremely nice person who was very kind to me had passed away.

If one's own currency could be measured by the number of smiles and laughs they created while here, I'd argue that Cindy left this life as the richest woman in the world.

Rest well, Cindy.

4

Henry Winkler

Actor, Author, Producer, and Director

But now, Ed, I think, wow, if I didn't have a learning challenge, maybe I wouldn't be on the radio talking with you.

***

There was a time when it could be argued that Henry Winkler ruled the world. His castle was the mega-hit television series *Happy Days*, his domain was Tuesday nights at 8 PM on ABC, and his subjects were the millions of television viewers who made Henry the top star in all of television during the second half of the 1970s. Henry turned the character of Arthur Fonzarelli, aka Fonzie or simply The Fonz, into a true pop culture icon that superseded *Happy Days*. If you didn't live during that time, you can't truly understand how "The Fonz" became a part of the American consciousness, so much so that his trademark leather jacket still hangs on display inside the Smithsonian Institution's National Museum of American History in Washington, DC. Also, the next time you're in Milwaukee, take a walk along the Riverwalk. You'll run into the Bronze Fonz, a public artwork that debuted in 2008, nearly a quarter century after the series ended its original run.

The second half of the '70s was not the greatest time in America. Our collective psyche was still bruised from the Watergate scandal, interest rates were high, inflation was even higher, and even gas lines returned during the final steamy summer of the decade. America needed to escape, and television was still a collective and unifying experience in those days. There were only three networks, which meant only three channels to find new shows, and even though we watched on giant 26-inch floor model color TVs, the shows we enjoyed still grew a bit wiggly and snowy at times because those favorite shows entered into our TVs via large skeletal antennas which stood proudly atop all of our homes and apartment buildings.

I was nine years old in 1976, and I had one as soon as the *Happy Days* lunchboxes arrived at my local Sav-On Drugstore. Thus, I would proudly transport my PB&J or cheese sandwich to Mrs. Karakatsanis' fourth-grade classroom inside John Marshall Elementary School in Edison, NJ. The smiling cartoon faces of Henry Winkler, Anson Williams, and Ron Howard would keep my sandwich protected each and every morning until 11:30. By the way, I'm just as shocked as you that I still remember not only my fourth-grade teacher's name but also how to spell it.

Thankfully, all that PB&J and cheese kept me healthy and growing so that several decades later, I could sit bright-eyed and bushy-tailed in the studio and await a call from The Fonz.

It was great to say hello to Henry Winkler.

The reason for Henry's visit with me on the show wasn't primarily to talk about *Happy Days,* it was to talk about Henry Winkler, the children's book author. Henry was celebrating *Stop That Frog,* the most current release from his *New York Times* bestselling *Here's Hank* series, co-authored with Lin Oliver. It is a series of books that, as I was about to learn, have quite a special and personal meaning for Henry.

"Henry, this is a true pleasure, welcome to the show."

Hi, Ed! Thank you for the invitation, thank you.

I immediately started our conversation with something I had read only a few hours earlier that morning, which, at first, truly surprised me. We all think of Henry for his work as an actor, but he's been quoted as saying that what makes him the proudest of all his achievements is the *Here's Hank* book series and its main character, Hank Zipzer. Henry confirmed it was true, and I then asked how his own personal struggle with dyslexia had evolved into a true labor of love with the book series.

Ed, the one thing that I say to every child that I meet anywhere in the world is that no matter how difficult school might be for you, it has nothing to do with what you can accomplish or with how brilliant you are. You've got greatness inside you. So, many years ago, Lin Oliver and I decided to write some Hank Zipzer books. We said, "Oh, you know what? We are gonna write for brand new readers, younger kids, second graders who are just starting their adventure in reading."

Henry didn't have the advantage of having any such books when he was young. In fact, he didn't realize he was dyslexic until the age of 31, as he was starring in *Happy Days*. That's quite a long time to have a problem and live with it without really understanding it.

"Henry, what was it like to finally be able to put a name on it and, more importantly, gain an understanding of your own situation?"

The first thing that happened was I was so angry because I looked back and I thought all of that yelling, all of that feeling bad, all of that punishment because they thought I was being lazy because I wasn't doing well in school, was for nothing because I had something with an actual name. But now I think, wow, if I didn't have a learning challenge, maybe I wouldn't be on the radio talking to you. The struggle literally kept pushing me forward so that I could have this wonderful life I'm living.

I could sense an infusion of angst in Henry's voice for ever so slight a second when he said it seemed that all he went through was for nothing. But that angst quickly seemed to evolve into a tone of affirmation when he talked about the struggle always pushing him forward. Henry Winkler is such a positive man, and it became palpable at this moment in our conversation. I then mentioned how, even with a learning struggle, he attended Emerson College and the Yale School of Drama and gave life to one of America's most iconic television characters.

I meet people all over the world who are pediatric surgeons, lawyers, sculptors, great plumbers. In every area of life, I meet people who have some sort of learning challenge. One out of five kids have some sort of challenge, and what I tell them is that it does not stop them from meeting their greatness.

Obviously, it did not stop Henry from meeting his own greatness. Even though *Happy Days* ended its original run back in 1984, it still lives on via streaming, on the digital classic TV channels that have popped up, and in YouTube clips. Henry has stayed quite relevant on TV, having played memorable roles in *Arrested Development, Parks and Recreation, Royal Pains,* and most notably in his role as Gene Cousineau in *Barry*. That role earned Henry an Emmy Award for Outstanding Supporting Actor in a Comedy Series. Very few actors have enjoyed such tangible successful relevance for that long of a time. But for a large portion of the American TV audience still to this day, Henry Winkler is Fonzie, plain and simple.

Happy Days aired from 1974 until 1984, but its heyday was its first five years on the air. After Fonzie literally jumped the shark and, by doing so, created a metaphor that is still used in our contemporary parlance, the show did begin to lose a little steam, especially after Ron Howard decided to leave in 1980 to pursue what would become a highly distinguished career as a film director. Donny Most also left at the same time. Ted McGinley was brought in to essentially take Howard's place, but it didn't have the same punch or appeal. Other younger actors were added to the cast as the original group was aging, but the flavor of the show was changing: Fonzie was now a school teacher and part owner of a rebuilt Arnold's after it was destroyed in a fire, plus he now had a girlfriend who had a young daughter. Too much change.

Also, in its first five or six seasons, a show that focused so heavily on looking and sounding like the later 1950s now looked nothing like it. All of a sudden, male actors had puffy, blow-dried hair parted down the middle, and even Marion Ross forewent her trademark late '50s, early '60s bouffant for a layered, feathered back, curling iron-inspired look during the final couple of seasons. The 1959 Milwaukee suddenly looked like 1982. Only Fonzie still looked the part, with the DA hairstyle and the leather jacket. Still, I was there every Tuesday night until the cast said their final goodbye at the end of the '83 - '84 season.

Those first five seasons, though, were incredibly special in terms of the large audience the show eventually drew after finding itself. I began my discussion with Henry about *Happy Days* by telling him the show ran from when I was 7 until I was 17.

"Henry, *Happy Days* was the show of my childhood."

Oh wow, Ed, thank you.

Now, as someone who saw every episode more than once, I felt reasonably qualified to go pretty far into the weeds with Henry when examining *Happy Days*. So, off we went.

"Henry, your character was very different the first year or year and a half. Fonzie was much quieter and even looked different, there was no leather jacket at first, instead wearing either a khaki or green windbreaker. What was up with that?"

Yeah, because you know why? ABC didn't want me to wear leather. They thought I would be associated with crime. So, I had to wear a MacGregor golf jacket, and let me just say, it was not easy being cool in a golf jacket.

"It's hard pretty much being anything in a golf jacket."

It's really true.

I told Henry that I've always believed the show found its stride in the third season, and I don't think it's a coincidence that it's when the show permanently switched from a one-camera format with a canned laugh track to shooting in front of a live audience. The decision to switch format came after a one-episode experiment by show creator Garry Marshall during season two. Henry explained what happened.

That was a last-ditch effort. We weren't doing so well with one camera, and ABC and Garry Marshall came up with the idea of doing one in front of a live audience. And if that didn't work, we would be off the air. Well, it worked, and in a very short amount of time, once we went in front of a live audience for good in 1975, we became number one and stayed that way for nine years.

"Henry, I remember hearing Ron Howard talk once about that first time you shot in front of a live audience. He said it was like being in a play and that all of you seemed to just feed off the energy which came from the studio audience being there."

That is exactly correct, and I'll tell you something: Ron had never worked like that before. I was trained in the theater, so to me, it was very natural. Ron never had done it and you would never have known it. It was like a duck to water. He was amazing and then became one of my most important acting partners in my entire career.

It's a bit ironic that *Happy Days* had a similar problem faced by another one of Garry Marshall's shows. A few years earlier, *The Odd Couple* used a one-camera format inside a quiet soundstage during its first season. Quite honestly, that first season of *The Odd Couple* could be labeled a tad boring and even a bit subdued. Once Marshall brought Felix and Oscar in front of a live studio audience and a three-camera format, the show improved greatly, and it seemed that both Tony Randall and Jack Klugman fed off their newfound energy.

In addition to Henry, who evolved into the unquestioned star of the series, the true strength of *Happy Days* was its main cast, especially the steadying influence of Tom Bosley, who played Howard Cunningham. I mentioned to Henry that I had seen it written that he considered Bosley as his acting mentor.

Yes, indeed he was, and Tom was like the real father on the set to all of us. If you had a problem with insurance, if you were buying your first house, you'd always go to Tom to talk about business, to talk about what to do, how to negotiate things.

It's an example of how close the entire cast became. They were so close they even had a traveling softball team. I grew up a huge New York Mets fan and was very excited when the Fonz, Richie, Potsie, Ralph, Joanie, and even Mr. and Mrs. Cunningham played softball at Shea Stadium in 1978 before a Mets game.

Ed, I still have the Mets bag I was given that day, and, by the way, Hank Zipzer, the character that Lin Oliver and I write about, is a Mets fan.

"Wow," I said, appreciating the irony, "Let's go, Mets!"

The traveling softball team allowed the cast to deepen their personal relationships outside of the regular, weekly routine of grinding out a show. They didn't just play at Major League ballparks across America, they went everywhere. The *Happy Days* softball team became a tool of global goodwill during a time when casts of American television shows didn't do that, and it solidified the idea that these characters, these performers, and this show, at least for a time during the late '70s, actually transcended television.

We traveled all over the world. We went to Japan, we went to Germany and played with the American troops over there. And still, as I travel across the country today, I meet people who come up to me, and they are now with their own children. They say, "We were there. I played softball against you in Okinawa in 1983." It really warms your heart that all of a sudden, there they are after all these years.

Plus, it must be noted that *Happy Days* spawned two other huge hit shows: *Laverne & Shirley* and *Mork & Mindy*, which introduced America to a young and at times frenetic comic actor named Robin Williams. *Happy Days* also spun off *Joanie Loves Chachi* and *Blansky's Beauties*, both of which failed miserably, thereby proving you can't win 'em all.

As I spoke with Henry about *Happy Days*, I realized just how much I not only liked but appreciated that show. Even while enduring occasional awkward growing pains and dealing with moments of family angst during those years, that show and those characters were always there for me on Tuesday nights at 8:00 on Channel 7. And I just realized as I'm writing this that perhaps that is the reason why I've had so many actors on my show who starred in *Happy Days*: Henry Winkler, Marion Ross, Donny Most, and Anson Williams, who has been on a couple of times. Wow, maybe it's time for me to call Dr. Melfi.

I could have talked with Henry for hours, but alas, radio segments are finite animals, and it was time to bid Henry adieu.

"Henry Winkler, I've enjoyed this very much, thanks for joining me."

Thank you, Ed, I've enjoyed it as well.

What struck me most in the immediate moments after speaking with Henry is how centered, how content, and how much at peace he appears to be. He is an incredibly gracious and kind man who seems genuinely appreciative of the obstacles he overcame, the career he continues to enjoy, and the life he continues to live.

Now *that's* cool.

5

Peri Gilpin

Actor

We knew it. We talked about it all the time about how we'd never find another job like this and we were very appreciative of it. It was lightning in a bottle

***

There are countless actors who never made it and never really got their chance to shine. There are also hundreds of actors through the years who have worked and continue to work quite often. They are the somewhat recognizable faces that you see and know, but you never learn their names. Factor in as well the hundreds of background actors you see filling scenes on network shows and films, who also practice their craft with speaking roles in small independent films. Yours truly fit that last category for several years prior to the radio show. Then, there are the few who, through talent, luck, karma, or whatever, score a role in a television show or a film that becomes iconic. Their place is firmly and permanently reserved in the higher echelons of the entertainment industry.

Sure, they may become a bit typecast after being so identified in a prominent role. Seriously, did you really ever buy into Carroll O'Connor playing a sheriff on *In the Heat of the Night* wearing that hairpiece and talking with a southern drawl? Sorry, but that's Archie Bunker from Queens, and he only wears un-ironed white dress shirts with black slacks.

I had the chance to speak with someone who achieved that status, where the role she rode into television history is recognizable to millions simply by hearing her character's name. Roz.

It was great to say hello to Peri Gilpin.

Peri was booked on the show, not mainly to talk about *Frasier,* but to talk about a new and much smaller project she was currently starring in. Immediately I was struck by how excited Peri was to chat about *Old Guy,* a new YouTube series about a man in his eighties who returns to acting after a 56-year hiatus, only to find that his choice of roles is somewhat limited. Peri portrays the octogenarian actor's agent. I asked her about how she became involved in the project.

Ed, this is made by a production company called Five Sisters Productions, and it's literally five sisters, two of which are great friends of mine that I've known for a really long time. They would tell these hilarious stories about their parents. It just felt like a natural thing to do because their parents were so entertaining. And then they said, you are not going to believe this. My dad retired from being head of psychology, I think at SUNY Buffalo, and he's in LA and auditioning for stuff. He's gone back to acting and he's like, on fire, but everything's like, you know, an adult diaper commercial or something where he's playing a cadaver. That's all he was doing. And so that made me laugh. They then sent me a script that they wrote about it, which I just thought was a natural progression for producers to do, to have a great story and then figure out how to tell it.

I then told Peri that I had watched the entire series, and I thought it was hilarious. I also told her I thought *Old Guy* was quite poignant because it tackled the subject of viable, vital people who are shunned from many parts of life, especially when it comes to employment, simply because of their age.

I think it's a great reflection of life right now," said Peri. *"We don't have much respect for our elders in the way that people used to and the way that other cultures do. I really love how this series addresses that. And I love that I got to be a part of it because I truly believe it. We're not listening, you know, we're actually listening to the wrong elderly people.*

Peri and I both enjoyed a good laugh about that last comment, and it should be noted that our conversation took place in late 2020, the waning days of the Trump administration. Anyway, *Old Man* was created to be a short-form series explicitly tailored for the YouTube audience, an audience that consumes its media in short spurts and, in many cases, on their smartphones as they go through their day. Actually, I'm included in that group as I watched an episode of *Old Man* while online at Walmart. I wondered if Peri noticed any differences working in a short-form series as compared to her long run in traditional episodic television.

None at all. But I have to say, I'm married to an artist. He paints paintings, and we talk about how he tells stories in one frame. I often tell stories in a lot more than one frame and all of it is valid. But each frame has to give you a ton of information and each line needs to as well. And the producers did a really great job here. I'm so glad you brought that up. There are stories that maybe would not be best served in this form, but for them to do such a good job this way, it just says so much about what you can do with this form of filmmaking.

I was so impressed by how excited Peri seemed about starring in a short-form series on YouTube. Her performance in *Old Man* was funny and top-notch, and she talked about it with me just as a young actor fresh out of film school would when talking about their first professional acting gig. She truly loves what she does.

It was then time to talk about her time on *Frasier*: 263 episodes over 11 seasons. It was one of the defining TV series and pop culture elements of the 1990s and its influence stretched nearly midway into the next decade as well.

"*Frasier* is not only one of the best-acted shows ever but one of the best-written shows ever. You talk about fine material. It was smart and funny, with characters that were completely fleshed out, and one of the best ensembles ever. Tell me what it was like to be a part of that for so many years."

Oh, it was an amazing experience from beginning to end. Every day was a blast. We knew it. We talked about it all the time about how we'd never find another job like this, and we were very appreciative of it. It was lightning in a bottle. I think we all really loved what the show was about, what it said, and its style. No one was miserable within that, and everyone was super happy in it. So, I think that's what made it lightning in a bottle, something that you can't necessarily create, it just kind of has to happen. Every day was fun because Kelsey wanted it to be fun; he wanted it to be a fun place to go work. He had nine years of experience doing that on Cheers. *So, he knew the elements it took to make it an enjoyable experience. Plus, with all the writers, you had about a thousand years of combined experience writing great sitcoms. And so, it was kind of like "peak sitcom." It truly was.*

Frasier had perfect chemistry and a unique pace. It was a show based on intelligent comedy, and you needed to pay attention to truly appreciate the wordplay and nuance within it. It's also a show that never lost its fastball. It didn't limp to the finish line the way some other legendary sitcoms did. I also appreciated the fact that radio was a key aspect of the setting and premise of the show.

"Peri, the workplace of the show revolved around radio, which for me hits close to home, and it actually changed talk radio. From the very beginning of the show, Roz, even though she was sitting on the other side of the glass in the control room often spoke on the air to Frasier Crane. At that time, that never happened on real radio. But now it happens all the time where producers chime in and talk to the hosts on the air. So, Roz Doyle was a trailblazer."

Robin Quivers was the only one doing that with Howard Stern.

"True, but Robin isn't the producer, she's essentially the co-host. Roz was the one screening the calls, putting folks on the air, running the board, and telling Frasier, 'We have Jenny from Seattle on the line, she's in love with her big toe.' What Roz did help change the talk radio world."

I then began to explore Peri's career outside of *Frasier,* which includes the field of voiceover work.

"You have also done a great deal of voice acting. It's so ironic. Last night, my son and I ended up watching a *King of the Hill* episode, and there you were voicing one of the characters. I was like, 'Wow, that's Peri Gilpin. I'm having her on the show tomorrow.' Peri, voice acting is great fun, isn't it?

Oh my God, especially with that gang of people. I had so much fun on King of the Hill. *I did a couple of them. I played a couple of different characters, and I loved that show. Plus, the writing was amazing. And Mike Judge actually did an episode of* Frasier *that was really fun. In it, we all had to have training in sexual harassment, and Mike played the guy that gave us the seminar. And yeah, voice acting is fun. It's a different kind of acting because you don't have to worry about what you look like when you're doing it.*

I then talked about perhaps why voice acting, and voiceover work in general, is so strong within Peri's DNA. Her biological dad, Jim O'Brien, worked for several years very successfully in both radio and television in Philadelphia.

"Peri, he had one of the best sets of pipes I've ever heard. So, I guess it's fair to say the vocal apple doesn't really fall far from the tree."

That's very nice, thank you. We're from Texas and he had an accent. I still have it. I remember him tossing a football while practicing his diction and practicing his elocution, and he put everything he had into that. One of the writers from Frasier, *Ken Levine, interviewed him years ago when he was out here because Ken also worked in radio, DJing and doing sports announcing. Ken sends me airchecks of my dad every once in a while. He was amazing, he was really good at what he did.*

Her dad was also an incredible workaholic. At one point, he did the morning show at WFIL Radio in Philadelphia, then anchored the noon news on TV. Later in the day, he did the weather on both the six and eleven o'clock newscasts and was back in the studio the next morning at 6 AM to do it all over again.

He was a workaholic. I think he just wanted to be able to do it all. The radio station and the TV station were affiliated and located in the same building. So, he just said, "I have a place next to the studio. Just call me when you need me, and I'll be there." He lived for it. He just loved it.

Unfortunately, Jim O'Brien's life came to a tragic and incredibly early end when he was killed in a skydiving accident in 1983 at the age of only 43. I then decided to do something with Peri that I tend to do from time to time with actors. I pulled up her IMDB listing, and I scrolled all the way back to the beginning. "The first thing I see for you is a 1988 episode of *21 Jump Street*, titled 'The Currency We Trade In.' Your character was named Fitzgerald. Do you remember it?"

Oh my God, are you kidding? It's like yesterday. It's how I got my SAG card. On the flight up to Vancouver, I remember James Woods was on that flight. He must've been going up there to work on something. When I got there, I felt so bad because I hadn't learned how to do handcuffs. And somebody said, "Don't worry you're not really a police officer." But sure enough, I had to cuff a guy a bunch of times, and I did not know how to do it. I think there might've been some bloodshed. So, I felt really bad about that.

"You drew blood?!?"

I think maybe that I did. I remember feeling terrible, but we were up in Vancouver for over two weeks because they ended up going on strike; Johnny Depp was there, and Peter DeLuise was my partner on the show, so I got to know everybody, and I got to know Vancouver. I remember it very well.

Now we know why when an actor works on a set and is about to be cuffed, they must sign a waiver releasing the producers of any liability if the actor cuffing them hacks their wrist off in the process. It's the Peri Gilpin rule.

Peri was a great guest, and we had a great conversation. I must admit it was a tad surreal to hear Roz Doyle's voice on the other end of the line. I felt a bit as if I was dolling out psychiatric advice over the radio, albeit without the aristocratic persona and accent.

I'm listening, Seattle.

6

Norman Lear

Producer and Screenwriter

Excuse me, Ed, what you're hearing is a little oatmeal that went down the wrong way.

***

The late 1960s presented quite a dichotomy in American life. Protests were common in the streets of our cities, our involvement in Vietnam was being seriously questioned and considered rudderless, and the spring of 1968 brought a period of 62 days which were book-ended by the assassinations of Martin Luther King, Jr. and Robert F. Kennedy. The network news dutifully created an electronic journal of those troubled times, but the troubles seemed to disappear once the prime-time television schedule began each night. The late '60s were awash with *Green Acres, Get Smart,* and *I Dream of Jeannie.* Yes, there was *The Smothers Brothers Comedy Hour* and *Rowan and Martin's Laugh-In,* but those were few and far between.

We escaped into an innocuous array of predictable "setup and punchline" sitcoms, song-and-dance variety shows, and light dramas. What we watched at night rarely reflected the events and mood of the country. Escapism is fine when used to momentarily deflect, but it becomes problematic when used to run and hide. Television of the late '60s had become the blanket that America pulled over its head. It was about to change.

As the decade of the 1970s began, television started to embrace a sophistication it previously shunned. Characters, especially female characters, became deeper and were developed with more layers of texture. Situation comedies began to matter. No longer did they just give us slapstick reasons to chuckle, but they made us laugh while awakening feelings and emotions about the issues of the day. All of a sudden, prime-time laughter had a purpose. The show that changed the course of American situation comedy and television as a whole was *All in the Family.* The person most responsible for that show is the one person who was extremely instrumental in television's growing up and realizing that we could both laugh and think at the same time.

It was great to say hello to Norman Lear.

Norman was in his late 90s when we spoke, and what struck me immediately was how strong of voice, personality, and conviction he was that day. It was heartwarming to hear just prior to our conversation that Norman was a regular listener of my show. As just some kid from New Jersey who grew up in front of a 19-inch color TV in the '70s, that was pretty cool to hear. It was time to chat with the man who changed what I saw on that TV.

Hello there, Ed Kalegi, it's quite an honor to be here, even this I get to experience, Norman said quite graciously.

I began our conversation by mentioning that by creating some of the greatest societal mirrors of his time, Norman proved that social change could occur by filtering it through laughter. I wondered how difficult that was to do. Norman immediately paraphrased H.L. Mencken: "Nobody ever lost money underestimating the intelligence of the American people." The establishment, in this case, the television networks, were slow to understand that the American people were ready to face their problems and that it was the right time. The networks were already showing via their news divisions what was happening in Vietnam, what was happening in our changing politics, and what was happening in our streets. Norman told me he and his writers decided to use their experiences, their everyday family lives, and what they read in the newspapers as they began to reshape television.

We were living through and dealing with all of these issues as well, Norman emphasized as he began to cough and then forcibly cleared his throat. *Excuse me, Ed, what you're hearing is a little oatmeal that went down the wrong way.*

Now, this is the greatest fear of any talk show host. Trust me, you don't need the guest becoming incapacitated or, God forbid, worse than incapacitated in the middle of an interview. Luckily, Norman merely got a bit too conversationally aggressive while enjoying that morning's divvy of Quaker Apples and Cinnamon. He quickly recovered, and I figured I'd ask: "I hope at least the oatmeal was good."

It was very good, said Norman, *but it's not as good as this conversation.*

With the oatmeal now securely down the Lear hatch, Norman explained that American audiences took to his shows because they were grateful to finally see the problems they were living. They could watch a show and afterward talk about the important subject matter. The works of Norman Lear were the gateway to conversations around kitchen tables at night, water coolers in offices, and lunch trucks on construction sites during the day. *Leave It to Beaver* could never stir America's conversational stew the way *Maude* did.

I then pivoted a bit in our chat and wondered if there is enough socially active television available now. Do we have a modern-day *All in the Family?*

Well, America's greatest product is excess, and we do have great television. replied Norman. *I'm sure it's the golden age, but there's so much of it. I still find myself going back to* South Park.

"South Park?!?" I chuckled as I was a bit shocked. I remarked to Norman that I never thought of him as a "Who killed Kenny?" sort of guy. Here was the dean of the modern American sitcom, the man who gave us many of the more indelible television characters of the later 20th century, admitting that *South Park* is where he heads first in what he feels is the golden age.

Yeah, after 25 years, they're still hard at it, and it's some of the best satire I've seen anywhere.

Lear's love of *South Park,* I believe, both personifies and precisely defines his scope. He always understood what was needed during any particular time to create conversations, skewer authority, challenge pretension, and entertain with enlightenment. While many may consider Trey Parker and Matt Stone, the creators of *South Park,* fearless in their satire during an age of strict political correctness, they at least followed Norman Lear's groundbreaking work back in the 1970s and others who piggybacked on Lear's Lewis and Clark approach to the sitcom dynamic. Lear was the canary in the coal mine; he was the Neil Armstrong of sophisticated television comedy. There was simply no one like him who preceded him. Carl Reiner receives a tremendous amount of credit, and rightfully so, for modernizing the American situation comedy ten years earlier with *The Dick Van Dyke Show.* But even though that show was more adult for its time, Rob and Laura Petrie still slept in separate beds, issues of the day were never truly discussed, and storylines were often still pretty bland.

Norman in the '70s had Carroll O'Connor and Rob Reiner screaming at each other about Richard Nixon and Watergate, while Carl in the '60s had Dick Van Dyke and Mary Tyler Moore somehow ending up singing and dancing in their living room during a dinner party. Both were considered groundbreaking, but they were so incredibly different in approach. Lear dared to go where no writer or producer had before, and once he did, there was no way television could turn back. Norman Lear changed his industry, an industry that had the power to change America.

While today's shows benefit from constant repetition of episodes, shortened clips popping up all over YouTube and social media platforms, and streaming on 89, oops, make that 90 subscription services, Norman's shows thrived in a world without the benefit of the current ubiquitous overexposure. In the 1970s, TV shows were just that - TV shows. They aired once at a specific time and place and usually one other time months later during the late spring or summer during the rerun season. Each episode had a much smaller window of opportunity to make its mark. Yes, Americans had fewer choices in terms of what they watched, but the quality of Lear's programs and what he was saying with those programs elevated his shows above the level of simple passive entertainment and brought them to a point where they became a part of the grain of not only our pop culture but our political discussion as well.

I had been thinking about having Norman Lear on the show ever since I visited the Smithsonian National Museum of American History some years before with my wife and son during a trip to Washington, DC. As we walked through the carefully arranged artifacts, I noticed something that shocked me at the time and still makes me shake my head in disbelief. Many of those who meandered along with us and looked to be in their 40s, 50s, and 60s gave a reverent but only semi-interested glance as they walked past the top hat worn by Abraham Lincoln that fateful night at Ford's Theater. But as we continued our explorative stroll from room to room with essentially the same people, I was amazed by what I saw as we entered a display of items celebrating twentieth-century American pop culture. Two old chairs sat at the far side of the room, carefully placed behind a vanguard of protective glass. In between those chairs, a small side table; on it, a generic can of beer.

As the same group who seemed only somewhat moved by Lincoln's hat saw the worn but familiar chairs and the table faded by a patina of age, they stopped in their tracks. Many smiled out of nostalgia, and a few actually seemed a bit moved as they all were presented with a part of American history that was instantly recognizable, tangible, and a part of their own history. It was Archie's and Edith's living room chairs from 704 Hauser Street. Norman Lear's work had found its place next to Abraham Lincoln's hat. It was Americana at its best.

Ed, I can't overstate how I love hearing that. It's a reflection of how they laughed as a family at something out of the fabric of American life, those characters and those subjects we were all dealing with.

One of Norman's most remarkable aspects was the number of sensitive subjects he and his writers tackled. Aspects of life that families at that time still seemed squeamish to discuss at the kitchen table became societal teaching points in Lear's primetime classrooms. I wondered if there was any subject, any topic that Norman wanted to explore on *All in the Family*, *Maude*, or *Good Times* but didn't. Norman paused, searched his memory, and then told me confidently that there wasn't. Everything he wanted to *go near* he did. Lear was still working within the parameters of what was allowed on 1970s television, and within that structure, he explored everything he chose to pursue.

I then mentioned to Norman my belief that the visceral reactions I witnessed at the Smithsonian also reflected how indelibly dug into the fiber and fabric of American culture his characters remain all these years later. People welcomed those characters into their homes every week and still live with the memories of those same fictional people. The example I cited for Norman was Edith Bunker. Norman took Edith to a place rarely examined and shown on television at the time when the episode "Edith's 50th Birthday" aired in 1977. In that episode, Edith escapes from an attempted rape by an intruder. It was a groundbreaking episode in many ways, which proved empowering for women and showed America's love for a fictional character brilliantly portrayed by Jean Stapleton. Legend has it that the actor who played the intruder was brought out in front of the studio audience prior to the episode's taping to reassure those in attendance that what they were about to see was simply an actor playing a role. America cared about Edith Bunker that much.

I was caught a bit by surprise when Norman then told me that the original script for that episode was not written for the Edith Bunker character. It was written for the role of Ann Romano.

Ed, we wrote that script with Bonnie Franklin of One Day at a Time, *a much younger woman in mind. We had read some stories about rapes where young women were perhaps inviting trouble by wearing short skirts, and we thought, wait a minute, we'll take this and do this on* All in the Family *where Edith is not a conventionally attractive young woman, who doesn't wear provocative clothing, just to show that this is what takes place in an average family.*

At this point, I came to a question that only Norman Lear could answer. "Norman, tell me what happened to Archie Bunker, finish the story." I think I surprised Norman because he first thought I was asking what happened to Carroll O'Connor, the actor who played Archie.

"No." I said, "The character of Archie Bunker, if you could script it, how did Archie end up?"

Oh, Ed, that is such a good question, such a good question, maybe that'll be my next show.

We both chuckled and then Norman took me into his creative mind, which always has its compass pointed towards using his art to expose our society's shortcomings.

Archie Bunker would be in his nineties, and he'd be very let down by the America he thought he was living in, thinking he could live on the money he was saving and Social Security, living in an old age which was promised to him but isn't happening for him and so many Americans now.

Thus, the magic of Norman Lear: someone who created activism, thought, and societal reflection through entertainment and characters that remain a part of our collective American family. Even though Lear made his biggest impact in the 1970s, the aftershocks of that influence can be seen and heard in the comedy and satire of today. It's great that several of the Classic TV-based HD subchannels that now dot the landscape of both streaming and cable are bringing Lear's shows back into a regular rotation and introducing younger generations to the original intonation of comedy with purpose. Norman Lear will forever be known as a pioneer in his field and someone who redefined our American conversation.

My conversation with Norman was at its end: "Norman, this has been quite a thrill."

My thrill, too, Ed; thank you so much.

Norman passed away on December 5, 2023, at the age of 101. His was a life well lived and one which left its mark in a very distinct way. I'm so very happy I had a chance to speak with him.

7

Brooke Shields

Actor, Former Child Model

Bummer I'm not being asked for those roles anymore.
I can be a prostitute! Uh, I can be sexy!
Please? Somebody? Anybody?

***

It's hard to believe in today's oversaturated media world that there was once a time when the most famous people in pop culture were relegated to prime-time television and both weekly and monthly magazines. There was no ubiquitous social media, no entertainment news shows, no channels dedicated to celebrity news, nothing. Yet, some created enough buzz or had enough buzz created for them, that brought them to the forefront of pop culture of the time. As I sat waiting for my next guest to call, I kept hearing the same line over and over in my head.

"Do you wanna know what comes between me and my Calvins? Nothing."

It was great to say hello to Brooke Shields.

Brooke and I are around the same age, so I remember her rise to fame quite well. It was 1978, and she was in a movie called *Pretty Baby,* and I remember younger adults talking about the film with a slight grin on their face while the grandmas and grandpas of the time discussed it with raised eyebrows while peering over the tops of their eyeglasses. In the film, Brooke, who was eleven at the time, portrayed a child prostitute. Even in the socially evolving and sexually expressive days of the late 1970s, the film still caused quite a stir.

The celebrity enjoyed, or perhaps endured, by the younger incarnation of Brooke Shields was shared with her mother Teri. So much so that Brooke and Teri appeared together on the cover of a 1977 edition of *New York* magazine. Teri carefully guided Brooke's professional career, a career that began when Brooke was only 11 months old when she was photographed for an Ivory Soap ad. A robust modeling career was launched, followed by a burgeoning film career. But it was *Pretty Baby* that cemented Brooke Shields into the brightest spotlight 1978 could provide.

Teri Shields was criticized by many during Brooke's younger years concerning how she was guiding her daughter's career and public life. So much so, the caption on that *New York* cover I just mentioned read: "Brooke is twelve. She poses nude. Teri is her mother. She thinks it's swell."

Brooke was coming on my show at an interesting time. She was on a media tour discussing her relationship with her mother, already deceased for many years, and defending her mother after what she felt was some harsh treatment shown toward her.

Ed, a major newspaper decided that instead of printing an op-ed piece that I wrote and paid my $1,500 for it, they, in a very sneaky and roundabout way, printed on their front cover a very scathing article and a review of someone that they had never met before. And when I realized the lack of humanity in that, the idea that there were no names attached, a girl, an only child who lost her mother, watched her die, was next to her, saw her take her *last breath. Why is that not at all respected? It was so interesting to me that there was zero thought or integrity in that.*

"Brooke, why do you believe they were so harsh? What was their motivation?"

I just think it's because much of the time the truth doesn't sell, you know, the intricacies of it. Because if they really took the time to care or understand, they would then have to look at their own lives. It's also just human nature. It doesn't sell if it's not sexy. If it's not tabloid enough, it's not interesting enough. The part that I had trouble with is decades after this woman was in the public eye, completely no longer relevant, nobody could have given a you-know-what about this woman for 30 years. Yet they still wanted to use her to sell their paper and put it online as well, to put something on their front cover about a dead person. That's the bully in the playground that sees the little kid with the broken leg and kicks him in the shin.

I mentioned to Brooke that it's the TMZ mentality we have today. We have so much media: professional, amateur, and social. The more salacious or scandalous it is, the more it stands out in an age where information, be it good or bad, is constantly being churned out.

"We're at a point where if Miley Cyrus or Taylor Swift makes a funny look in the supermarket line, it's huge news."

True, but if it's intended, then to a certain extent, she succeeded because we're still talking about it. But I don't think I necessarily would've survived what I did if it was happening in this era because of the access to social media and because, you know, anything goes now. There used to be a modicum of respect surrounding journalism, you know what I mean? And yet, on the other side, it could be argued that, to a certain extent, my mom created the first reality star.

Brooke Shields had just read my mind. Teri created a career for the pre-teen and teenaged Brooke, which, when viewed through a modern prism, could be considered a "reality" star. Perhaps, even a bit Kardashian-esque. Except Brooke actually worked in films and did things. The jury is still out on what exactly any of the Kardashians have actually done in the entertainment industry other than a very repetitive and seemingly highly choreographed reality show. Obviously, though, strong opinions would be voiced during any era about a child actress posing nude at such a young age, especially when the child's mother was so closely guiding her career.

"If you take your situation, Brooke, and if you put it nowadays, the amount of attention it would get would be staggering. The spotlight can be difficult for anybody to deal with at any age, and for you personally, you were in it in a huge way. You were eleven in *Pretty Baby*, and of course, coupled with the idea that you played a child prostitute, your mother was criticized."

Brooke then abruptly snipped off my last syllable and quite effectively added some deadpan humor to our conversation.

Bummer I'm not being asked for those roles anymore.

"Wouldn't that be a fun phone call?"

I can be a prostitute! Uh, I can be sexy! Please? Somebody? Anybody?

"See that; we're making news right here, ladies and gentlemen of the entertainment world, Brooke Shields..."

...the oldest prostitute ever, said Brooke, completing my sentence.

"There you go, if you're looking for an older prostitute, call Brooke Shields now!" We both enjoyed a good laugh, and I think we were both surprised at our Abbott and Costello-ish comedic timing. However, I did want to return to the question I was beginning to pose. "Brooke, your mom was criticized back then for some of the choices she made for your career. Was that criticism fair?"

I think any criticism is fair because it's someone's opinion, and people love to say, "Would you let your daughter do what you did?" Well, the opportunity hasn't arisen, and we're in a different period. It is not as bizarrely safe as it was in a very sick kind of way. But what people seem to keep forgetting is that I got the opportunity to work with one of the foremost auteurs of cinema, Louis Malle. This was an artist who had been so recognized creatively and was already legendary. What I was so angry about, even as a kid, was that I couldn't believe they had demeaned it so. It was a true story. It was so beautifully filmed. My day-to-day on that set was not salacious, and I hap-

pened to have been creating a long-lasting piece of art, and it didn't stress me out.

We then talked about an infamous appearance Brooke and her mom made on *Donahue.* A staple of the show was that the second portion of any interview was essentially Phil running around with a microphone and allowing the audience to ask questions and comment however they chose. Brooke remembers it quite well.

People stood up, and they were screaming at my mother, demanding to know, "How could you do that?" My mother, granted, she was hungover, and that's a bigger issue, but she stood up and said, "I'm sorry, ma'am, have you seen the film?" And the woman said, "Well, no, I would never see such smut." And my mom said, "Okay, why don't you go see it? Then I'd love to have a conversation with you." It was amazing and it was kind of a cool thing.

Brooke then talked about her mom keeping her in a bubble. She never read any material about herself, not a review, nothing. She admitted to me that if she had read anything negative, she *probably would've shriveled up and died.* Brooke eventually saw it and read it when, at 35, she was cleaning out some boxes that housed that material from all those years before.

I couldn't believe what I saw. I instantly felt hurt and angry, I felt less than...and I felt like I was a horrible actress. And I mean, this was just from reading these things, you know, years and years later.

There was palpable emotion in Brooke's voice, and I wanted to finish my conversation with Brooke on an up note. I still had one thing remaining on my list of bullet points I wanted to bring up with her. It was the elephant in the room. It was *The Blue Lagoon.*

"Brooke, I have to go here. *The Blue Lagoon,* you and Christopher Atkins are marooned on this island, but the makeup always looked perfect. Your hair was always styled perfectly. You had that fresh Wella Balsam look. Tell me, was there a Great Clips somewhere near that lagoon that we didn't know about?"

Well, that was tens of thousands of dollars worth of hair because it was really natural hair. It was waist-length and wavy hair, and people had sold their hair to make it. The first day I put on that long wig, nobody took into consideration that possibly a wig might not have the same life in it that my own hair did. So I dove in the water and basically came out with a rat's nest, and we had to go on hiatus for about a week until they got me another wig.

That was truly a going into the sausage factory to see how the sausage is made moment for me. And I find it more than a bit humorous that Brooke chose to describe a wig that cost tens of thousands of dollars to create as a rat's nest. That's why, folks, always be sure to ask interesting questions because you'll always get interesting answers.

As we ended our conversation, I felt that Brooke truly enjoyed it. I sure did. She was incredibly cool to talk with. I came away from our time together feeling that Brooke is very comfortable with the woman she is today. She never strayed very far from the entertainment industry and became quite successful outside of the early hullabaloo of the choices her mom made for her career. Brooke Shields is a woman with perspective and a healthy understanding of her own story. She also loves her mom very much and I sense she misses her very much too.

Brooke and I attended college around the same time, but we were only 17 miles apart: she was at Princeton, and I was at Rutgers. Alas, there was never a reason for her to travel north up Route 27 and me south down Route 27 to have that chance meeting. But, as I did then, I still have those Calvin Klein commercials wedged in my memory from all those years ago. Okay, now I'm blushing.

Please, go on to the next chapter already.

8

Rosanna Arquette

Actor, Director, Activist

What's really important for me is to be a voice for the voiceless.

***

One of the true privileges and welcome responsibilities of hosting a show such as mine is the opportunity to discuss true matters of importance. Normally, the show doesn't rely on the headlines of the day to determine the guests. But when something truly moves the needle of the national conversation, I not only want to discuss it, but I feel an obligation to do so.

The MeToo movement exposed a systemic culture of sexual abuse and sexual harassment. It empowered many women to tell their stories. In the entertainment world, many of those stories shared a similar thread: Harvey Weinstein, the co-founder of Miramax, was sent to prison after being convicted on charges of rape and sexual abuse. One of the more prominent and consistent voices exposing Weinstein and the culture that enveloped Hollywood is Rosanna Arquette. Her crusade to create awareness and a platform for women to feel safe to tell their personal stories became a defining moment in the MeToo movement.

I had received an email from a Los Angeles-based publicist asking if I'd be interested in having Rosanna on the show as she was promoting a new film. Considering that, at the time, there were countless media stories about the MeToo movement, I said I'd love to have her on the show, but chatting with Rosanna Arquette about a new movie instead of the impact of MeToo would be akin to having Neil Armstrong on the show in late July of 1969 to ask if the Tang really tasted like orange juice. It would've been tone-deaf. The publicist agreed, as did Rosanna, and we set a date for her to come on the show.

It was great to say hello to Rosanna Arquette.

"When you hear the phrase MeToo, you think of her," I began, "Rosanna Arquette, welcome to the show."

Hi, it's so nice to be here. Thank you, Ed.

I used the word *pioneer* in my opening comments, and I believe properly so. Many would trace the true nexus of the movement to an article penned by Ronan Farrow, which appeared in *The New Yorker* in October of 2017. One of the women featured in his groundbreaking piece was Rosanna Arquette and the story of her encounter with Harvey Weinstein. I started here with Rosanna as I thought it would be a good place to begin our short conversational journey together. I mentioned how it's quite amazing when one thinks of the groundswell that article created and what has occurred since. Many things, including attitudes, have changed.

"Rosanna, how has it changed for you?"

Ed, I hear every day from women who have been so afraid to speak out, to come forward with their stories. It's given a lot of people hope and strength to be able to tell their stories, even though they've been living in shame and fear for so long. So that's really been something for me, that I have found myself really here just to help other people tell their stories, and maybe that's what this all is about for me, standing behind the women who have been abused, especially by Harvey Weinstein.

Given the fact that articles are published every day, many, if not most, of them evaporate and leave little impact. The Farrow piece was different; it loosened the valve on an overheated steam pipe that had been ready to blow for quite a long time, one filled with frustration and inner torment. At the time of her interview with Farrow, could Rosanna even imagine it would have the impact it did? She told me that, more than anything, it was still a time of intense fear. This is not only for her but also for all the women who have decided to speak with Farrow. Rosanna explained that until then, no one listened or she had been politely told to shut up. This was also the case for the other women profiled by Farrow. But as the story took hold and garnered meaningful attention, Rosanna said it's now giving people the strength to come forward, tell their stories, and be fearless in their fear.

It's a chain reaction. One story opens the door for someone else to tell their story, and it goes on. So, I always feel as if we're all holding hands across the world, all women.

As I listened to Rosanna, one word presented itself front and center in my mind: catharsis. These women, for years, were told to essentially stay in their lane and endure the unendurable, even after being abused. It must be uplifting to have an environment where one can feel free within one's industry to speak the truth, tell one's story, and liberate one's inner spirit. Not only that, but to see people finally held accountable, and in the particular case of Harvey Weinstein, convicted and sent to prison. That feeling of vindication, that feeling of relief, that feeling of catharsis must be incredible. But as I spoke with Rosanna, I began thinking of the entertainment industry as a whole. There aren't many communities as progressive and socially active as the collective we know simply as Hollywood. Considering the show-business industry's persistent activism on many other issues, I had to ask Rosanna a question.

"The entertainment industry has been so progressive on other issues, so socially active through the years, but when it came to this, it lagged behind so terribly. Why do you think that was?"

I think because people were afraid of losing their jobs. I think many people were complicit in protecting people because of their paychecks. There are a lot of powerful people, really what it is. These things are all horrible abuses of power. The light is now being shown in darkness, and that's really what's happening here across the world, across the board. They wanted to shut us up, they wanted to shut us down, but it's not going away. It's just the truth. The truth will always rise to the top, and that's what's happening.

Rosanna Arquette has a history of turning the spotlight around and shining it on Hollywood itself, not to glorify but to expose and educate. I thought back to when she directed *Searching for Debra Winger,* which examined ageism and sexism in Hollywood. I wondered how important that film was, in context, as a precursor to what eventually happened with the MeToo movement. Rosanna told me it was the opening of a door, but she quickly added that when the reviews came out, there were some in the Hollywood trades that were not favorable and a few that were quite horrible. One in particular, which appeared in *Variety,* was extremely scathing. Ironically, that same day, the film received a standing ovation in Cannes. After the screening, women were seen crying, and Rosanna was congratulated by director Alexander Payne, who told her the film was terrific.

Searching for Debra Winger made its debut in 2002. As Rosanna told me about the negative reactions to the film, it made me realize that our world, now more than twenty years removed, is a much different place. Have we, as a society, matured?

"Are we simply now just more socially able to handle certain subjects and topics? Have we evolved in a good, positive way to a point where now we can deal with certain issues?"

I pray that we are evolving. I hope that that's the case, but also, with social media, no one can get away with anything at all. You have instant access to exposing people's crappy behavior. You see racist behavior, ranting on buses and trains, and it's being exposed immediately, and you know who this person is. You can't, you can't hide under a rock anymore. You can't pretend like you're a good person and then do these horrible crimes, which really are a crime against a woman or a child's soul. It's interesting when I'm talking about this. I'm feeling my own anxiety rise in my chest, and I'm talking to you about it, getting tongue-tied and going, wow, it's, it's trauma. I'm talking about a lot of people's traumas that I carry around with, you know, people that I know that are close. My experience with Harvey was not rape, but it was an abuse of power and did affect my life in a huge way and career.

As our conversation developed, I wanted to be sure I maintained the comfortable environment for which I had promised Rosanna. I decided well before the phone rang in the studio that afternoon that she would lead me into talking about her encounter with Weinstein, not the other way around. As she had just mentioned the experience and hinted at the effect it had on her career, I decided to explore that.

"You have talked about your encounter with Weinstein back in the early '90s, at the Beverly Hills Hotel, where he pressured you to touch him. You said no and left. As you were leaving, he said, 'I think you just made a big mistake.' You've also talked about how once you were back down in the lobby, you said to yourself, 'Watch how my career is gonna take a hit because of this.' Rosanna, you knew it, didn't you?"

I just knew it. Yeah, I felt it in myself because, at the time, he really was the king. He was the most powerful guy, and the thing about him, and the only nice thing I'll say about him, is that he had really good taste in films. He made good films, but for me, it was never an issue as I was never going to go down that road with him. He did say two names to me: 'Look what I've done for so and so and so and so, and they're big stars.' I also think that he lied about that. He said people ended up winning Academy Awards because of it. That's not true! It's not true at all. He used that! He would use that and say: 'Look what I did for her career,' and I don't believe it was true. I know women who certainly never made a deal with him to further their careers. I mean, they were young girls who were raped.

As we talked, I kept trying to wrap my mind around an industry and culture where an individual had such extreme hubris and bravado to make such demands of women and expect full and immediate cooperation. I also kept thinking of that time, a time when it was impossible to think of Harvey Weinstein ever having to pay for his actions and his crimes. I then thought of those who were victimized, and since Rosanna had become a brave voice for the collective, I figured she would be the perfect person to answer my next question.

"When I hear your story," I began, "and I see what's happened with this, and I see him being taken away in handcuffs and brought to trial, I have to ask: in the middle of the night when you're lying there in bed, and you think about this, do you ever get to the point where you just simply exhale and say, 'we got that bastard'?"

No, I don't. Unfortunately, I wish I could feel that. Two days before the arrest, we all were talking to each other, keeping in touch because the anxiety was so high. Finally, you have justice for those who were raped and for the lives that were shattered. But you don't come back from things. The women who I know were raped are still in trauma, and it is trauma that can destroy a person's psyche, and people are hanging on by a thread sometimes.

I must admit, I was saddened by her answer. I didn't expect her to respond with a rousing "Hell, yeah, we got him!" But I was taken by the sobering tone that still governs Rosanna's voice when she talks about what Weinstein did and the damage he inflicted. Justice can punish the guilty, but it cannot completely heal the guiltless. Some wounds simply scar over in an ugly way and can easily be ripped open again at any time.

Considering how front and center she had become in the overall MeToo movement, I was compelled to tell her that, at this point, I now think of her career and her activism on the same plane.

That means a lot to me, thank you very much, Ed.

"Well, it's very true. Let's say fifty years from now, someone hears the name Rosanna Arquette, and they go look in the history books.

Well, we won't even have books then. It'll be some digital thingy or whatever."

At this point, she abruptly interrupted me: *You make me so sad because I love books!*

I told her as we briefly detoured that I love books too and that I can't really do the digital thing. I need to hold a book in my hands, take it to bed (to read it), take it on a plane, and have it as I settle into the recliner in the living room. She agreed that reading a book should be a tactile experience as well. She added she needs the book "grounding" her. My response was that she and I were kindred spirits, and I told her about all the reading I must do to prepare for the dozens of authors who appear on the show. I admitted that I've tried to read off my laptop, and then, when lying in bed, I close my eyes and have that white square that I can't get rid of. It's terrible.

Oh, Ed, it's really bad for your eyes. We have to fight for bookstores to stay open and support them. I always go to my great bookstore in my hood and come home with a pile of books. I have to say, unfortunately, they are piling up more than me reading them, and that's making me very sad. But I read so much when I'm on holiday.

I then admitted that one of the things I love most about books is that, after reading them, they make terrific decorations. I have several bookcases filled with books in my home studio, which I love. Anyway, I then completed the question, which I felt was key to our conversation.

"Again, take me fifty years from now," I posed. When someone thinks back to Rosanna Arquette, do you want them to think of you as an actor, director, and producer first or an activist first? Which means more to you?"

I would definitely say activist. What's really important for me is to be a voice for the voiceless. I mean, there are so many people who are not able to speak out and have a platform to be able to do that. That's what's more important. It's not about me. It's about if I have access for other people and to support them, their stories, and their voices. That's the most important thing.

We all leave a footprint in this world, but it's how indelible and meaningful that footprint is that matters most. I connected that with the beginning of the MeToo movement and told her that everyone knows what MeToo is, what it truly symbolizes, and is so encouraging considering where it can go from here. She agreed and expanded on the thought.

I think it's even transformed to not just the individual being safe enough to come out with their story, but it's WE Too, and within it all the MeToos are holding hands with the WeToos, and we've become the We Too movement all across the world. All of us are able to connect with each other, and someone who's feeling marginalized and worried and could never come out and talk can now do so. There's a safe space, a tribe of women that are there for them.

The individual voices that for such a long time were never heard are now all being heard and have created a chorus of power and change. It's quite a step forward and an even more impressive evolution. Our conversation had ended with the perfect crescendo, a true message of hope. It was time to say goodbye, and I thanked her for joining me.

Thank you so much, Ed, and I really appreciate everything you do for women.

Coming from her, that's quite a compliment. Thanks, Rosanna.

9

Lorraine Bracco

Academy Award, Emmy, and Golden Globe, Nominated Actor, Screen Actors Guild Award Winner

When we finished the pilot, David Chase opened a bottle of champagne. I looked at him and Jimmy and said the Tony Soprano-Dr. Melfi scenes will either be really good or the weak link in the show.

***

Actors strive to create lasting characters, characters that transcend their respective films or TV shows, and find a familiar place in our collective conversation and culture. An actor is extremely fortunate to be able to do that once, they are quite blessed if it happens twice. I had the chance to speak with someone who, in fact, has accomplished it twice, with her portrayals of Karen Hill in *Goodfellas* and that of Dr. Jennifer Melfi in *The Sopranos.*

It was great to say hello to Lorraine Bracco.

I had the pleasure of speaking with Lorraine during the successful seven-season run of the TNT crime drama *Rizzoli & Isles,* where she appeared in all 105 episodes. At one point during its run, the show topped the charts as basic cable's number-one series and built itself a very loyal following. I asked Lorraine why she thought that was.

I think it's because of Angie Harmon and Sasha Alexander, and their relationship, and what they do. You've got the smart, wise detective and an incredibly educated medical examiner, and it's just the juxtaposition of their relationship. The girls are smart, they're witty, they're hip. They are a joy to work with.

I discovered an interesting irony in that *Rizzoli & Isles* was a show rooted in blending the work life with the family life of both the overall plot and the characters. That was the essence of *The Sopranos* as well. I mentioned to Lorraine just how much better TV has become, and that is primarily because HBO decided to push the envelope of what episodic television could be. It has forced everyone else to raise their collective bars in what they do.

This is truly the era of television. There's no doubt about it. People were tired of the same formula of television, and they wanted something different. I believe the public has gotten much smarter.

I agreed with Lorraine and added that television has become much more nuanced and sophisticated, especially with crime shows. There was a time, especially during the '70s when a crime show was essentially a white guy wearing a sports jacket with creased gabardine slacks chasing two other white guys around for an hour who were dressed in three-piece suits and patent leather dress shoes. During that time, TV made it seem as if Los Angeles was 98 percent white, 96 percent male, and 93 percent between the ages of 42 and 51. Ironically, *Sopranos* creator David Chase succeeded with this approach as a writer and producer of *The Rockford Files.* I love *Rockford* and feel it was James Garner's best work, but fortunately for the medium and the audience, Chase upped his game big time years later when *The Sopranos* hit the small screen.

Lorraine's two iconic roles were cemented into the culture's consciousness during the '90s, one at the very beginning of the decade and the other near the very end. First came 1990's *Goodfellas,* where

Lorraine scored an Academy Award nomination for Best Actress in a Supporting Role. Lorraine's portrayal of Karen Hill, a Jewish woman from Long Island who became an all-knowing mafia wife, made her a star. I ended up reminding Lorraine something about her character that I had just discovered the day before we spoke.

"Lorraine, I just learned something I never knew. I now know what Karen Hill's maiden name was! I never knew it was Freedman!"

She let out a huge laugh and admitted to me she had forgotten what Karen's maiden name was. She then said that it was written that Karen's grandfather was a Rabbi and that she was brought up in a very strict Orthodox family. Now you can see why all my research pays off. You can go on with your life knowing that Karen Hill was initially Karen Freedman. You know you'll tell that to at least three people later today. Anyway, back to Lorraine. I asked her how she got the role in *Goodfellas.*

I knew Martin Scorsese.

"Well, that's a good person to know."

I knew Martin socially, and I've been told basically that it was always my role.

Honestly, that's the type of career security any actor would kill for. I then mentioned how *Goodfellas* is one of those films that whenever you stumble across it with your remote, you know you're now going to stay there and watch it all the way through. There are so many iconic scenes and lines. I had to tell Lorraine about a famous Karen Hill line that still pops up from time to time in my home.

"Even now, all these years later, when I'm at home, and my wife sees a spider, and I have to kill it, and I ask what happened, she goes, 'I just got scared Henry. I just got scared.'" This brought about the loudest laugh any guest has ever had on the show. It was truly a belly laugh.

Wow. Okay, that's cute.

I told Lorraine that story because it's proof of how certain lines from iconic films and TV shows permeate our everyday language.

Goodfellas has at least ten or fifteen lines that fall into that category. We moved on to talking about *The Sopranos,* which debuted on HBO near the end of the '90s on January 10, 1999. I began by asking about something that is reasonably well known at this point, that David Chase wanted her to audition for the part of Tony's wife, Carmella Soprano, but for Lorraine, that was a bit of a been-there-done-that type of thing. She wanted to read for the part of Dr. Jennifer Melfi.

I just felt that with Goodfellas behind me, I don't think I could have done it better. Jimmy was a fascinating actor. I feel very, very blessed that I was able to work with him in that way.

"What I always enjoyed most about your scenes with James was the one-on-one dynamic. It was so unique because most of the work that you did on that show was with James, and it was almost always set in Dr. Melfi's office. That is such an exercise in acting. You were able to explore those characters in such a different way year after year after year when it was simply just the two of you. The element of that relationship between Dr. Melfi and Tony Soprano, in that office, had to be so interesting and exciting to be able to explore the craft of acting in that way."

Well, the truth of the matter is, when we finished the pilot, David Chase opened a bottle of champagne. I looked at him and Jimmy and said the Tony Soprano-Dr. Melfi scenes will either be really good or the weak link in the show.

"Really?" I was quite surprised. "Why did you feel that way?"

People sitting across from each other talking does not usually make great TV.

"But, Lorraine, it was *great* TV."

I believe she was being a bit modest and perhaps unnecessarily so. I think once the quality of TV began to improve, the sophistication of the audience quickly followed. As the writing modernized and dealt with subject matter worthy of the times it served, an appreciation developed for a level of acting that, until then, had never really been seen on episodic television. Viewers were ready to be challenged. *The Sopranos* came along at just the right time.

Yes, I believe that.

As did many others, Lorraine received four Emmy nominations for her work in *The Sopranos*. As the series progressed, the character of Dr. Jennifer Melfi deepened and broadened. We learned she had an ex-husband, a family, and her own need for therapy when she began visiting her own therapist, played extremely well by legendary director Peter Bogdanovich. Perhaps, though, Lorraine's most brilliant performance in *The Sopranos* was in the season three episode "Employee of the Month," when Dr. Melfi is sexually assaulted and considers asking Tony for his professional help. It is an amazing performance.

We then spent a moment talking about another part of Lorraine's life, her earlier years long before *Goodfellas*, when she was a fashion model, beginning when she moved to France in 1974. I commented to her how that must have been a very interesting experience.

Well, I lived in France for 10 years, and it was, uh, you know, I always said I went to France as a girl, and I came back as a woman.

We both laughed, understanding the saucy irony that cradled that comment. I told Lorraine that outside of her colorful quip and considering her young age at the time, it's still a wonderful way to come of age and experience a different culture and different part of the world.

It was great, a fantastic experience, and yeah, I'm fluent in French.

If we had more time, I would've asked her how to say "I just got scared, Henry, I just got scared" in French so I could update the repertoire at home, but alas, it was time to bid au revoir to a fun and gracious guest.

Thank you, Ed, for having me. How lovely this was.

And yes, about an hour after I got home that night, my wife asked me to kill a bug.

We really need to call an exterminator.

10

Chazz Palminteri

Actor and Producer

I think the story of* A Bronx Tale *holds and endures because it talks about things that really mean something in life. I think all people can relate to that.

***

Every artist yearns to create that signature piece, something that is instantly recognized and always associated with them. It could be a painting, a piece of sculpture, a sheet of music, a stage play, or a film. If the artist achieves such a creation, it may very well become his life's work and his definition.

From time to time, I've had the pleasure of speaking with incredibly talented people who have each molded their signature pieces and given them to the world. One of those people is someone I found to be extremely comfortable in his own skin, extremely humble, and quite a nice guy. His signature piece? *A Bronx Tale.*

It was great to say hello to Chazz Palminteri.

As I sat in the studio waiting for Chazz to call, I wondered what would be the perfect introduction to the audience. Since *A Bronx Tale* has contributed many memorable lines to our everyday pop-culture-based language, I figured that would be the perfect way to begin. The phone in the studio rang. I answered, and it was Chazz. We chatted for a few moments before officially beginning our conversation, and I was struck by how friendly and engaging he is. I knew who he was, he knew who I was, and we talked like old friends resuming an old conversation. Soon, it was time to begin recording the segment for my show.

"My next guest is responsible for one of the most beloved stories and screenplays of the past few decades. When you hear phrases such as 'no worse thing than wasted talent' or 'now you can't leave,' and if you've ever wondered whether or not she'll lean over and unlock the driver's side door, you think of one thing: *A Bronx Tale*. It is great to say hello to Chazz Palminteri. Chazz, welcome to the show."

Well, thanks very much, Ed. Thanks for having me.

I told Chazz the main thing I've always taken from *A Bronx Tale*, from the very first time I saw it in the theater back in 1993, as well as every time I've watched it since, are the lessons which are learned from it. Family is everything. Family doesn't necessarily have to be a blood relation. Learn to protect yourself. Learn who to stay away from, and finally, sometimes, the world around you tries to dictate how you can feel and even who you can love.

"Chazz, these are some extremely powerful things."

I think the story of A Bronx Tale *holds and endures because it talks about things that really mean something in life. I think all people can relate to that. The relationship between a father and a son, a father and a daughter, telling your children not to waste their talent. Do something with your life. Don't make it a failure. You know what I mean? So, I think all people can relate to that. It's a cautionary tale. It also talks about racism. It talks about how racism is bred in you. You're taught racism; no one's ever born a racist. So, it has all these elements about my life.*

His life? Chazz's life? Yes, for those that still may not realize, Chazz's real name is Cologero, as in the name of the main character in *A Bronx Tale,* the young boy who grows into a young man while the world around him changes and changes him at the same time.

I am Cologero, said Chazz; that's *my real name. My name is Cologero Lorenzo Palminteri. That boy you see is me, and I wrote about my life growing up in the '60s.*

What we all see whenever we watch *A Bronx Tale,* or if we see the Broadway musical or Chazz perform it as a one-person show, is an actor and a writer who is recreating a much earlier part of his life. We all have memories of our childhood and our adolescence, but we never have the opportunity to schematically rebuild it and literally present it to the world. I mentioned to Chazz that it must be a surreal feeling to tangibly participate in bringing one's own memories back to life in a very unique way not to mention recreating the people who have been in that life.

Ed, what was really amazing was Robert De Niro hanging out for a month before we filmed because he wanted to learn about my father's ways and about how he drove a bus. It's pretty exciting to see how Robert De Niro plays your father. Talk about the ultimate actor.

"And the film was De Niro's directorial debut," I chimed in.

That's true. I also remember my mom and dad first seeing the film and seeing their lives up there and their son. It was pretty...

Right then, Chazz paused. I got the impression he was immersing himself in that moment, and for a brief second, I could hear emotion in his voice. He then completed his thought.

It was pretty, wow! I still think about it sometimes once in a while.

I then took Chazz back to 1989, to the creation of *A Bronx Tale.* It was at Theater West in Los Angeles, and when the world first witnessed Chazz's creation, it was a one-person production. I told Chazz that I have some acting experience in my background, some film and stage at least enough to generate an IMDB listing, and the thought of performing all of the characters, male and female, in *A Bronx Tale* is incredibly daunting. Yet Chazz was able to capture the essence of these individual characters and morph from one to another with both precision and grace. I struggled for a more intricate question, but all I could summon was the obvious. "Chazz, how did you do that?"

You know, it's funny you say that because most people who have seen the film or the musical go, "Wait a minute, wait a minute. I don't understand something. You mean you did this on stage by yourself?" And I go, "Yeah." They say, "You just talked." I say, "No, no, no. I played all the parts, I did the whole play and movie by myself on stage." Yeah, I played all the parts.

"Chazz, how difficult was it, at least at the beginning?"

I just had this idea about doing something like this. I started doing it and it was really, really hard when I was first starting. I mean, I was very frustrated, but I kept working at it, and I rehearsed it for about a year until I had it right. And then when I put it up in LA it just exploded. It won all the awards. It took off just like Hamilton *broke the boundaries in musicals. It was kind of like I broke the boundaries of one-person shows because no one ever did a one-person show like this. Usually, in a one-person show somebody talks, they tell you about their life, they do a character, then they talk to the audience. But this was a movie straight through. Ed, it made me a star, you know, it really did.*

Hollywood took notice, and now it seemed everyone wanted Chazz's story, but there was one problem.

When it became so hot, everybody in Hollywood wanted it. Every director, producer, and studio wanted to make it. They offered me $250,000 when I had $250 in my pocket plus $200 in the bank. And I refused because they didn't wanna put me in it. They said, "Look, you're great, but nobody knows you." I told them I wanted to be in it and write the screenplay about my life. They still said no. Then they went up to $500,000, and again I said no. And then another studio came in, and they offered me $1 million. Again, I said no, I want to be in it.

It's very hard to turn down that kind of money when you have only $450 to your name, but I guess it's harder to turn down your heart. Ultimately, listening to his heart paid off because about two weeks later, Chazz returned to his dressing room after a performance and found someone waiting for him.

I walked in, and there was Bob De Niro. He said, "Wow, this is the greatest one-man show I ever saw. It's a movie, and I want to do it. I know what you want so I'll tell you what I'd like to do. You should play Sonny. You'll be great. And you should write the screenplay because it'll be honest. It's about your life. I'll play your father and I'll direct it, and if you shake my hands, we'll go partners." And that's how it happened.

Wow, even the most far-fetched daydreams aren't as perfect and fleshed out as Chazz's impromptu meeting with De Niro. Obviously, things worked out, but it's quite a testament to Chazz believing so much in himself, his project, so much in his desire to be a key part of it, and to steward it to the screen with both care and dedication. I don't know if I could've held out as Chazz did if someone had offered me that kind of money to simply take a check, cash it, and hit the beach in Malibu.

Chazz's success as an actor and director has allowed him to pursue other interests, specifically as a New York restaurateur. The Chazz Palminteri Italian Restaurant is located on West 46th Street in the Broadway theater district. The success of that location has spawned another one, located just north of the city in White Plains. It's not a coincidence that when scanning the menu, one will find a dish called "A Bronx Tail." It is lobster tail with clams, mussels, and shrimp, sauteed in a light spicy tomato sauce, served with homemade fettuccine. Chazz has always enjoyed operating the eatery, but it was extra special during the twenty-month run of *A Bronx Tale: The Musical,* which played in a theater only three blocks from the Manhattan restaurant.

Ed, it's an amazing thing because I go to my restaurant a lot, obviously because I'm in the city a lot. And when the Broadway show was running, people came to the restaurant, they saw me, they'd say, "Oh my God, we're gonna go see your play." Then they would come there after the show, and they would go, "We just saw your play." It was an incredible experience. You could truly have a Chazz Palminteri experience!

As we were chatting about the restaurant, I pulled up the menu on my studio monitor. The food looked wildly inviting, and all of a sudden, I became quite hungry.

"Chazz, as you know, I live and work in New Jersey, and as I look at the menu, my taste buds are ready to leap from my mouth and drag me through the Lincoln Tunnel and up to 46th Street. These dishes look phenomenal."

I have to tell you, I have one of the finest Italian restaurants in the city. We make great steaks and pasta; we make our own pasta. Everything is fresh. My name is on it, so it has to be. The food is really amazing, and we have a great chef. He buys the stuff every day, and the restaurant is doing great. It's really fantastic.

At this point, I was torn between going into the city for a great Italian meal or going home to watch *A Bronx Tale* for the 37th time. But before I decided on that, it was time to bid Chazz farewell. "Chazz, it's been an honor to have you on the show. You're one of those guests I can now scratch off my proverbial bucket list."

Ed, that's so sweet of you. It's my pleasure, thank you.

Chazz Palminteri: actor, director, restaurateur, and a man who has lived his life in defiance of his father's famous credo: "There's nothing worse in this world than wasted talent."

Chazz definitely did not waste his.

11

Gwen Carr

Activist, Public Speaker, Author

We have to protect the children that are coming behind my son. I advocate so strongly to have this not happen to another family.

***

Ever since I began hosting the show, I realized and understood there is a great deal of responsibility tethered to the privilege of having a program with your name on it. Obviously, it is a duty to entertain, and I think that's been accomplished. I also believe there comes a time when certain stories grab our collective attention in such a profound way that I need to explore them. This demands a greater responsibility and also the intellectual curiosity required to explore so that maybe the show can enlighten and educate in any way it can.

July 17, 2014, was a warm summer day on Staten Island. A 43-year-old man by the name of Eric Garner died on a Bay Street sidewalk not very far from the Staten Island Ferry terminal. Garner died at the hands of New York City police officers as he was being apprehended for the alleged crime of selling "loosies." Loosies are cigarettes sold on the street individually from their original pack. Garner was wrestled to the ground while having a prohibited chokehold applied to him by Officer Daniel Pantaleo. With several officers pinning him to the ground, Garner was heard saying, "I can't breathe."

That three-word phrase uttered eleven times would be the final 33 words ever spoken by Eric Garner. After Garner lost consciousness, he remained lying on the sidewalk for seven minutes before an ambulance arrived. About an hour later, Garner was pronounced dead at a local hospital.

Losing a child, even an adult child, is one of the most heartbreaking and sobering challenges in the human experience. It turns the circle of life counterclockwise and is disturbingly unnatural. These were some of the thoughts that ran through my mind in the studio as I awaited my next guest. This would be a very different conversation from others on the show, but one which was necessary in a very precise way.

It was great to say hello to Gwen Carr.

Gwen joined me to talk about her book, *This Stops Today: Eric Garner's Mother Seeks Justice After Losing Her Son*. It's a poignant read that details her newfound role as an activist, a role in which she seems incredibly comfortable. It is her way to continue fighting for her son, as any parent would do. A number of years had passed between Eric's murder and my conversation with Eric's mom. I asked Gwen if the passing of time had given her any additional perspective on what happened to her son as well to those responsible for his death.

Well, we did have a departmental trial that brought out a lot of things that people didn't know and that I didn't know. But in light of things, we did get one police officer fired, even though there were at least six involved that day. But it's a step in the right direction. I just thank the public for standing behind me, those who did stand behind me, I thank the groups that I joined with. I thank them for standing behind me, and I thank God.

Daniel Pantaleo, who applied and held the chokehold in place, was the officer fired by the NYPD. It took five years for Pantaleo to lose his job. "Gwen, why do you believe it took so long for the firing of Pantaleo?"

I think it took so long because I don't think that the administration did what they should have done. Once they saw the video, those officers should have been fired right away because there was no doubt that it was murder. But that didn't happen. And they dragged their feet for five years. Even the Department of Justice, the DOJ, came into play, and they decided to drop the ball and not go forward with charges. And they did this on the anniversary of the fifth year. So now I was back to square one, but I decided to go forward, and that's how I got the departmental trial. And that's what I tell everybody: you just can't stop pushing because the push is against you. You have to push forward.

What struck me most about Gwen as our conversation developed was the tender grace that she displayed blended with the tremendous amount of resolve she communicated. Here is a woman who watched her son being murdered by police. She saw this on television, replayed over and over, as did millions of others. She watched a death that was unnecessary and essentially witnessed police act as judge, jury, and executioner. Yet, she herself has arisen to become a voice against oppression.

"You have pushed forward, Gwen. You have become a tremendous advocate and quite an activist. You have spoken on Capitol Hill, and you helped further a conversation in America, which is a very necessary conversation for you personally. How important is it for you to take what happened to Eric and try to make a positive difference with it?"

Well, we have to turn pain into power because there are so many of us out there who are suffering the same pain that I am, and no one has even heard about them or knows them. So, they are the faceless and the nameless. We have to stand up for them. We have to protect the children that are coming behind my son. I advocate so strongly to have this not happen to another family.

I then told Gwen how, after seeing what happened to her son, I've often wondered how many other Eric Garners there have been. The only reason the world knows what happened to Eric is that someone recorded it on that fateful day. Thus, how many other Erics were there, those who didn't have their murder recorded and then shown to the world? My question may have been a bit rhetorical, but Gwen didn't answer it that way.

There are thousands. Eric Garner is not an isolated case. There are so many others that didn't get caught on video and that got swept under the rug. No one even investigated those cases. This is why we have to throw a light on it. People who do have the platform have to share it with others because we have so many mothers who are in the same state that I am, and they can't even get out of bed in the morning. They're on strong medications, and some have even tried to commit suicide. So, we have to help these mothers. We have to help people so they need not suffer this pain.

I couldn't help but focus on the word "pain." Nothing can ever really take away Gwen's pain. However, I could sense Gwen has been able to take that pain and her controlled inner rage and mold both into a resolve of purpose and pursuit of justice. It was interesting, too, that my conversation with Gwen took place not very long after the murder of George Floyd, and I mentioned to her that something really did seem to change in our nation during that time. There was justified outrage when Eric Garner was killed, yet the opinions of the country seemed more galvanized, and those opinions were rooted more deeply in a frustrated anger after the murder of George Floyd. Yet another inherent needless act of fatal brutality forged an enhanced evolution of enlightenment. I asked Gwen why things were different in the summer of 2020 as opposed to the way they were in 2014, after Eric's death. Gwen provided a very interesting take.

Ed, I think it's different because when my son was murdered, there was a big uprising. But now, when George Floyd was murdered almost the same way, only with the knee, it just sent a boomerang back to when my son was murdered. Except this time, the world was made to stay home because of the pandemic. They were made to look at what was going on in the world. Before, everybody was going about their busy lives. They weren't taking time to see what was happening, but now they were made to see how wrong we were being treated, that there was not only Corona (virus), but there was corruption. Now the world is saying, well, I'm going to take a stand because this is not right, and I'm so glad to see so many young people who are standing up, so many people of different races, different creeds, different religions who are standing up and saying this is not right. Once we bring awareness, we go from demonstration to legislation and this is how we are going to try to get the problem solved. It's not going to be solved all at one time, but one step at a time, and I just hope it's in my lifetime.

I then mentioned to Gwen that what surprised me this time, during the George Floyd protests during the summer of 2020, was that for every ten black people you saw at a protest, you saw ten white people as well.

Absolutely.

Plus, there were more young people at these protests than ever before. A lot had changed in the six years between Eric Garner and George Floyd. Gwen explained that she's experienced younger white people coming up to her and asking what they can do to affect change.

I tell them to talk to their peers and talk to their mom and dad, and one young lady said, "Well, my mom and dad just don't get it." But I told her to just keep talking to them and let them see what is going on, and if they see the history of what's going on, maybe they will pay attention like she is.

But now, along with the awakening of a more thoughtful and progressive younger generation, we've even seen corporate America rise to the occasion and involve themselves in a positive conversation concerning race. When the NBA returned to playing games in the late summer of 2020 within a Covid-protected environment inside Walt Disney World, players were wearing long-sleeved shirts that read "Black Lives Matter," and the court itself was emblazoned with that three-word phrase which became such an important part of not only the American lexicon but part of a larger and global conversation as well.

We then talked about systemic racism and how we've lived in a country where, for decades, we would wring our collective hands when it came to race relations but never really do the necessary work to completely combat the embedded social mores that insulated the gears of systemic racism.

I believe that no one is born a racist. I truly believe this. No one is born a racist. It has to be taught and embedded. This system is what has embedded deep-seated hatred and racism in people, and they don't even know why they hate.

I agreed and took it a step further. "You look at a kindergarten class or preschool class," I began, "kids of all different races get along, and they play with each other because they are simply other people. They are humans. But once they're exposed to certain things and the way older people around them talk and behave, they begin learning about mistrust, and it corrupts their minds. And it's a shame that it happens that way."

It does, Ed. It really does.

Gwen then mentioned something which was the most poignant moment of our conversation.

I remember when my son was young, and he was filling out a paper to send in to be able to buy something, and on the application, it asked his race. He said, "Ma, how do you spell human?" I asked why, and he told me, "It says race, and I want to put human race."

"Wow," I said when I obviously should've said more. "That's really beautiful when you think about it, Gwen. He was right. That is OUR race. We are all humans, and on the inside, our blood is red, we all have a heart, we all have bones, and we all have a soul. It's amazing how we've come so far in terms of medicine and science and everything else, yet there's still this one damn thing that holds us back: the color of our skin."

I then wanted to allow Gwen the chance to tell my audience about Eric Garner, the person. We all witnessed his last moments on Earth, but I wanted to allow Eric's mom to tell us about her son and the person he was. "Gwen, what do you want the world to know about your son?"

I would want them to know that Eric was a gentle soul. He was a caring person. He loved his family. He always loved to go out and be with family. Christmas was a big thing for Eric, and even after he grew up, he used to tell me about all the toys he remembered getting while growing up. It was beautiful that he could remember this, and he could reminisce about all the good things that had happened to him in life. He even told me one day, "Mom, you gave us a good life."

I could hear Gwen seeing Eric in her mind as she told me this. A mother's love never goes away; it is eternal. Nor do memories fade. They are our link to those we love and who have completed their time in this existence, be it if they are taken from us naturally or if they were taken unfairly, unjustly, and unnecessarily on a sidewalk in Staten Island.

"Gwen, I have to tell you this," I said. "Yesterday, I was in the grocery store, and there was a man in front of me, and he was wearing a T-shirt with the phrase, 'I Can't Breathe.' I immediately thought of our conversation today, and I thought about how God chooses us for different reasons and for different things. Yes, Eric couldn't breathe that day. But look at the breath he has now instilled in all of us to work to make sure that this crap stops once and for all. Gwen, your son Eric lives in all of us who yearn for fairness, justice, and equality. Sometimes angels are made in very different ways."

Yes, I believe that. Thank you for that.

I told Gwen it was both an absolute pleasure and an honor to have her on the show. It was a necessary and quite wonderful conversation. And I'd like to think that, somewhere, Eric thought so, too.

12

Cassidy Hutchinson

Former White House Aide
during the Trump Administration

I took my job believing my fidelity and my loyalty was solely to the country; at some point, it subconsciously went to Donald Trump and Mark Meadows.

***

It was a brisk and annoyingly raw early fall day in New Jersey as I was preparing for my yearly trip to the West Coast. I head to Los Angeles each year to meet with some of the publicists who provide the steady stream of great guests I have the pleasure of speaking with and recording a handful of in-person interviews while in Tinseltown. As I was packing, I checked my email to see who was being pitched to appear on the show after I returned from my trip. As I scrolled and read, my eyebrows suddenly lifted in great interest. Cassidy Hutchinson was appearing on selected shows and networks to discuss her new book, *Enough*, and the powers that be wanted me included in that group. I recently saw her on CNN talking with Jake Tapper and late one night with Jimmy Kimmel. But there were some things I wanted to ask Cassidy about, so I arranged my time with her, and her bestselling book arrived by courier the next morning. Thus, it was time to prepare for my upcoming conversation with Cassidy, and I would do so during two coast-to-coast flights over the next week.

Ten days after returning from Los Angeles, it was time to talk with a former Trump administration White House aide, a woman who had become a household name at the beginning of summer in 2022.

It was great to say hello to Cassidy Hutchinson.

It is one of the strange phenomena in our American culture and existence that certain individuals are thrust into the true center of our collective attention from time to time. Many times, it's because the circumstances surrounding them drive them quite unwillingly into that proverbial spotlight. A half-century ago, a pale and somewhat soft-spoken bespectacled White House Counsel named John Dean sat in a smoke-filled hearing room on Capitol Hill and found himself emanating from transistor radios and Zenith Super Chromacolor television sets all over America. In 2022, it was Cassidy Hutchinson's turn, only this time it was in a smoke-free hearing room and streamed to the world via smartphones and 52-inch flat screens, with clipped segments embedded into social media and YouTube posts where, digitally and on-demand, her images and words now live forever.

I was one of the millions who watched Cassidy's appearance before the United States House Select Committee to Investigate the January 6th Attack on the United States Capitol. I watched as a young woman, who seemed quite measured yet extremely focused on her purpose, methodically and with perfect cadence, described a time of great chaos and horror. Cassidy Hutchinson was detailing how democracy can begin to come apart at the seams. It was compelling television and presented in a way where it could not be ignored or misunderstood.

As Cassidy's appearance before the committee concluded, she rose from her chair, and the cameras stayed on her as she left the Cannon Caucus Room. Meanwhile, back in Metuchen, I was stretched out on my couch, wondering what she must be thinking at that moment as she left that room.

Fast forward sixteen months and I had the chance to ask her first hand. "Cassidy, what were you thinking as you left the room that night?"

Ed, I think there were no thoughts going through my mind at that point, to be honest with you. I think the thoughts started racing through my mind the moment I crossed the doors into the holding room. It's sort of a paradoxical experience to describe because on one hand I had been overcome with a sense of peace once Liz Cheney and I began in our dialogue that day, but I also was racked with nerves. But, when I crossed into the holding room, I was very proud of what I had done. I also was thinking, okay, what's next? I sort of began worrying and I also just remember feeling so tired.

The committee's presentation to the nation was structured in a way where the information and facts of what happened that day and the chronology of what happened built to an impressive crescendo, and Cassidy's testimony became its foundation. The evolution of Cassidy Hutchinson from loyal Trump White House aide to a conscientious American concerned about protecting the sanctity of free elections and the preservation of democracy was on full display to millions. But as I watched Cassidy, I kept wondering also what was occupying her mind, not necessarily as the insurrection was occurring on that cloudy and cold early January afternoon, but that night, as order was restored and our collective wound of what we now know as "January 6th" was still stinging, and freshly bruised.

"That night, in your heart of hearts when outwardly you were still 'part of the team,' who or what did you feel let down by the most?"

That's a really good question. I think there are multiple answers to that. I think my very honest answer is, at that moment, I felt let down by myself that I hadn't done more, that I had been complicit, that I had been witness to the most egregious attack on the Capitol and on our democracy in my lifetime and in modern American history. But I also felt extremely betrayed as an American by Donald Trump for what happened that day. It was a para-

doxical experience, which is sort of odd to explain, but I also still felt a sense of duty to him because at the time I felt that what happened on January 6th was the fault of the staff. I felt that it was our fault the former president was fed information that wasn't truthful and that if we had done a better job informing him that it wouldn't have happened. Now, of course in my hindsight, he is completely to blame for what happened that day. As an American, I knew that he had betrayed the Constitution and betrayed his oath of office but that was really hard to come to terms with that night.

I then turned my focus to Mark Meadows, Trump's Chief of Staff, that fateful day. Cassidy was instrumental, and many would argue that she was key to Meadows performing his job. It was reported only a few hours before my conversation with Cassidy that Meadows had agreed to cooperate with Special Counsel Jack Smith. Thus, the conjecture at that point was that Meadows could flip quicker than a pancake on the griddle at Denny's. With Cassidy's work relationship and acquaintanceship with Meadows now firmly in her rearview mirror, I wondered what her feelings towards Meadows were.

"Cassidy, do you feel anger towards Mark Meadows, or is it frustration or, perhaps, disappointment?" Right then, there was a pronounced pause in our conversation which lasted more than a few seconds. I started to think we lost our connection. Then, she spoke.

Ed, I realize I might get some heat for what I'm about to say here and I hope that I phrase it correctly. I have spent a lot of time and, thank you for asking this question, I think you're the first person to ask me this. Truthfully, I don't feel any of the above for him. Maybe this is the young, naive idealist in me, but I personally feel that hate or frustration or anger aren't really productive emotions. Of course, I have been upset by him and upset by what I have at least perceived to be his lack of action at points on this because I knew Mark to be a man that thought of himself as a man, a man of God, and he cared about the country.

Cassidy seemed to be choosing her words extremely carefully at this point. She had given a fair number of interviews during this time, but maybe my question struck a chord and caused her to drill much deeper into her feelings. Her tone turned more pensive, and I could tell she was explaining to me not only how she felt but, more importantly, why she felt the way she did.

I think it's important to always extend grace to people, and for me, harboring those emotions doesn't do anything productive. I would just hope that Mark would move forward in his life and recognize that he owes it to the American people to uphold the oath that he swore to protect and defend the Constitution and the country, and not to Donald Trump. Ed, my story is full of decisions that I'm not proud of, but it's also full of a salvation and a grace that saves my life and my future. And I want to be somebody that is able to extend that to people and not ever hold a grudge because I think that it's not productive. It's not productive, in my opinion, to chastise people for the decisions that they've made if there's still room for them to make the right decision. And I hope that people involved in this see that there is something that's much greater than politics at stake. We are looking at the future of our country.

Cassidy seems to have gained a perspective that allows her to, perhaps, not excuse the actions taken leading up to and during the insurrection itself but to create a way forward for herself. She was searching for a doorway that opens into the future and allows passage over the threshold of accountability. That threshold for her was her testimony to the J6 Committee. When we spoke, she was hoping others in general, and Mark Meadows in particular, would cross their own personal thresholds to a redemptive promised land.

"Cassidy, would I be wrong in saying that the people who worked in that administration, even at the highest levels, became victimized by the pervasive attitude that existed within the Trump White House and in all things Trump World where you sell out your soul for the good of Donald Trump? I really don't want to use the word 'victim,' but I'm searching for an appropriate perspective on those who were on the inside, were those people victims of the situation that existed?"

I don't like to characterize it necessarily as a victimization because it's a conscious choice. It's a conscious choice that I made. At one point, I took my job believing that my fidelity and my loyalty was solely to the country. Then, at some point, it subconsciously transferred to Donald Trump and Mark Meadows. At another point it became conscious and it took a while for me to come to terms with that. And when I did, I was disgusted with myself, but there was still room for me to correct course. But what I will say is either for people that are in Donald Trump's circle or even people that are his supporters or consider themselves as potential supporters, there is a sense of fidelity to him as a human being. And I think that when you enter that place in the American political system where you idolize a person, we start to enter dangerous territory because we can't put faith in a man. You have to put faith in the system that they promised to uphold and keep.

At this point, Cassidy's tone seemed to harden.

Donald Trump, time and time again, has shown us who he is, and I made the mistake of not listening to the warning signs that were glaring in the past. I see it as my obligation, my duty to do what I can to help open people's eyes so they understand that it's not just about the Republican party anymore, it's about our democracy. And Donald Trump poses the single greatest threat to our democracy in modern American history.

There it was: Cassidy Hutchinson's mission statement and her clarion call to the nation she believed she was serving. It wouldn't have taken Rembrandt or Dali to paint the portrait of delicious irony, which displays how her true service to America took place long after she surrendered her lanyard and key card to the West Wing. This seemed to be the perfect time to go a bit further and pivot to the state of the Republican party in the autumn of 2023, a party for which Cassidy has expressed her frustration.

"I remember Republicans from a generation ago," I began, "people such as Bob Dole and Jack Kemp, Bush 41 and Bush 43. These were principled men who were conservative Republicans. They respected democracy and the proverbial public square of discussion, debate, and decorum. I've heard you say that you no longer recognize this current, still very much Trump-led version of the party. What disappoints you most about that?"

I think what disappoints me most about it is that our system is designed to elect people of integrity, people who are supposed to be truthful and uphold their oath, and even if Donald Trump were to fall off the face of the earth tomorrow, there are problems that are permeating through the Republican party today that wouldn't just vanish. It is disappointing that these people that we have elected to represent the American people feel so beholden to Donald Trump that they're not doing their job or upholding the oath that they swore to and defend the Constitution. We also need to take a good, hard, and long look at our institutions of government and recognize that it is our responsibility to elect people who are smart.

Cassidy then talked about her part in electing people who are smart, and it was interesting to learn that she planned to help those who wear red and those who wear blue.

Ed, it's not just partisan. I hope to be able to help give a platform to smart, sensible Republicans and Democrats. We can elect a Congress that can be productive, and we can have those productive conversations like the great men that you just mentioned: Bob Dole, the Bushes, where we can actually have productive policy debates and get to a place where we're not debating whether or not the Republican party is becoming a fascist regime. We can debate substantive policy matters that will affect and hopefully positively impact the American people.

That's quite a statement. This young woman who was raised Republican in Pennington, New Jersey, and who worked Republican on the biggest stage possible just told me there is a legitimate question about whether "*the Republican party is becoming a fascist regime.*" If that is not an indictment of Trump World and all its tentacles, I don't know what one is.

It was time to bring our conversation to a conclusion, yet it would be hard to match the crescendo it had just achieved. I wanted to put Cassidy's contribution to our nation in a proper historical perspective, yet I needed her help in doing this.

"Cassidy, the next several generations of your family will watch your appearance in front of the committee, as will all of us. It's kind of the same way we now watch that faded videotape of John Dean from 50 years ago. As the passing of time jumps into the fast lane, and whenever people do go back and watch what you did and watch what you said to the J6 Committee, what do you want them to remember most about you?"

I think it is tricky. I want people to remember this moment in American history. I guess, sort of by nature, they'll remember me, but I want them to remember this moment in American history. I want them to remember somebody that stepped up when a lot of people weren't, and I don't say this from a self-deprecation standpoint, but it shouldn't have been me in that chair that day. I don't regret it, and I am glad that I did. It was an important conversation to have on a national level to help begin to open people's eyes to the dangers that Donald Trump posed and the gravity of what happened in that time period after the election. It was a period where there was a severe lack of accountability and people were avoiding subpoenas and hiding under executive privilege. And it took me sitting there that day to really call attention to the travesty of that. I think that if I can help restore accountability to our system, I would consider that a success in my eyes.

While only in her mid-twenties during the time of her testimony, Cassidy Hutchinson's personal story has many chapters still to be written. It will be interesting to follow Cassidy's path should she decide to live, work, and serve in a public life. Yet, no matter where that path leads, there will always be that time back in the summer of 2022 when she assumed an unwanted spotlight and shed true light on a disturbing and distorted time in our ever-fragile American Democracy. In that respect, she does share a rather strange commonality with the man in that faded videotape from so many years ago.

Cassidy Hutchinson and John Dean both sat with the eyes of the nation focused upon them as they took their individual stands against power gone corrupt, power on steroids, and men who each believed that they were more important than the nation they were elected to lead and the Constitution they swore to uphold. The age of Nixon and the age of Trump represent two very different times in America. In the nearly half-century that separates the two, our politics have become more divisive, our arguments more personal, and our extremes more dangerous.

We owe a collective and patriotic debt of gratitude to those who are willing to stand up and give voice to reason and sanity when it is needed most, those who expose lies and stand up for truth. Cassidy Hutchinson is one of those people. I was very fortunate to be included in that select group of journalists and media personalities who had the chance to speak with her.

Truth matters.

13

Jim VandeHei

Co-Founder of *Politico* and *Axios*

You have to adapt and adapt fast, particularly in the professional world, if you want to succeed.

***

Perhaps the most important part of my job as a talk show host is to make the best use of my words. Those words need to have a purpose, and they need to be carefully selected. Most importantly, I need to maintain an economy of words, especially today as attention spans continue to shrink. If I truly wanted this book to match its contemporary moment, I probably should've selected a handful of phrases from a half-dozen celebrity conversations, printed them on a pamphlet, and had it slid under your front door.

Our world is now governed by short, to-the-point communication. Be it a quick text to a friend, a trolling social media post, or an email to your boss, we are now expected to make our point with reasonable precision and crispness.

Jim VandeHei gets it. He is a renaissance communicator of the modern age, understanding how information needs to be conveyed, processed, and marketed. As co-founder of both *Politico* and *Axios*, he has helped refine how news is presented and consumed. He is the proponent of something he calls smart brevity, a concept useful not only for those in media but also for anyone who needs to communicate effectively in our modern world of constant communication.

It was great to say hello to Jim VandeHei.

As I began my conversation with Jim, I told him I was already concerned about becoming too verbose and asked him to reel me in if I morphed into a proverbial chatterbox. He chuckled, said I didn't need to feel insecure, and agreed to keep me in check. Just to make sure, I kept the internal Kalegi Word Count function fully engaged. I mentioned a quote of Jim's where he talks about how people reward you if you respect their time and intelligence in a world full of noise. I wondered why even the most educated and articulate people still seem to misunderstand this.

The way I look at it, responded Jim, *is most of us have lived in a world where you didn't have to think very much about the efficiency of communications, pre-internet, and pre-mobile phone. People had a little bit more time, and many of us were taught to be long-winded. Our teachers were guilty of instilling an innate long-windedness in all of us. They were the ones who required essays and compositions be written containing "X" number of words. We became conditioned to think, if you were an author, the bigger the book meant the smarter you were. If you were an academic, the longer the paper meant the better it was and the stronger your thesis.*

Jim then talked about how modern forms of communication, such as texts and social media posts, have created the need to use words efficiently. There is no need to constantly use SAT terms or acronyms simply to impress or show off how smart one is. In fact, just the opposite is needed: true written communication efficiency for someone to remember what you have said.

I asked Jim that, considering the environment in which we live, where we have content coming our way from 28 different directions at any one time, and when our attention spans are stretched to their elastic limits, why do we still seem to overly extend our verbal thoughts? There is still an urge to mention fifteen points when only three will suffice. I've known people who simply cannot verbally take me from point A to point B. It becomes this long trip out to points C, D, and E to places where even the buses don't go. Why are we our own worst self-editors?

You put it brilliantly. Foggy communicating reflects foggy thinking. It's important to prepare to communicate and to organize thoughts and words. Remember, you're communicating because you want someone to know something or to remember something, so make it easy on them. The key is to decide what is the most important thing you want to say, then distill that idea into the fewest number of words possible. Finish with context and show why it matters.

Jim said that when writing, it's important to stack your ideas into an order of priority and maybe even break them into bullet points so it's more pleasing to the eye. He believes these are tricks that can make you, as the writer, better remembered. If you communicate in the 2020s like you did back in the 1990s, it simply doesn't work.

People are not reading like they used to. They're skimming and they're scanning, and the war for their attention is intense. You're competing against Twitter, Facebook, Tinder, and other apps. It's a mess out there.

VandeHei feels that with all of the alerts, texts, and emails constantly coming in, anyone looking to communicate, particularly in the professional world, must adapt fast to succeed.

The number one thing is just stop being selfish. Stop writing and communicating for yourself and start writing and communicating for the other person that instantly clarifies things that instantly takes away a lot of the words that you would otherwise use. You would be much clearer if you were respectful of them. You'd be much more efficient if you're being respectful of them if you can just take that one step. And then there's things you can do. It doesn't need to be overwhelming. I think one of the reasons we communicate inefficiently is, and, and we often vomit words, is because we're so insecure that we haven't sharpened what we actually want to say. Be confident in the message you're trying to convey. If you can do that, then the rest of it flows more naturally.

I then remembered a *New York Post* headline that grabbed a great deal of attention when it first appeared back in the 1980s and is still referenced today: "Headless Body in Topless Bar." It was simple and sure did get its point across. I reminded Jim that he recently said he is a fan of short words because short words are strong words. They grab people and tend to stay with them longer. He agreed and said he believes the average writer can learn a lot from headlines. They can both accurately and provocatively grab someone. He believes the modern equivalent of the tabloid headline of yesteryear is the subject line of the emails and the texts we all send every day.

Grab me! Say something interesting, bring me into your story. Strong one-syllable words work. One-syllable words are better and more memorable than two-syllable words. Don't use fancy words, ones you wouldn't use sitting in a bar while enjoying a beer with a friend. The key is to be as simple and direct in both verbal and written communication.

I then pivoted to what paid the VandeHei mortgage and probably allowed for the purchase of more than a few nice cars: *Politico* and *Axios*. Both are excellent examples of relatable communication of information. It can be argued that *Politico* brought the coverage of key issues and Washington politics to a much younger generation, a generation that migrated to an interest in politics much earlier than those who preceded them. *Politico* has engaged that audience in a way that legacy media never really could. *Axios* has taken news coverage from the "Voice of God" era to one that is much more conversational in nature, aided by a sleek and intuitive visual design much better suited for the digital age. VandeHei told me his previous experiences working for huge legacy media brands churned his creative appetite to modernize journalistic communication.

Ed, I was trained in the Voice of God, I worked at the Wall Street Journal *and the* Washington Post, *and I was that stuffy writer. I saw it, and I lived it. What I realized most in doing* Politico *and in doing* Axios *is how people responded. Whether you're a CEO or a student, you respond to people writing more conversationally. That doesn't mean dumbing it down at all. It just means writing more conversationally. Not writing like, I'm superior to you and taking on this sort of, I'm writing from the mountain, and I'm chiseling it into a tablet. No one speaks that way. People want to have a conversation. And that's all communications and reporting is.*

Axios *is a massive company of 550 people now. We reach millions of people. The big discovery we made was the efficiency of information. That's what distinguishes us from the* New York Times *or* CNN *or even* Politico, *which we created before* Axios. *We obsess about the efficiency of information and being respectful of your intelligence, respectful of your time. That's what we did; the more we did that, the more we started to hear from companies, teachers, and school systems asking us to teach them to communicate the way we were communicating with readers.*

It's hard to disagree with someone who started two foundational contemporary digital media brands, brands which have, in many ways, redefined both journalistic style and approach. VandeHei's two media creations have managed to carve niches that stand out from the barrage of content that bombards us. The success of *Axios,* in particular, shows us that there is a market for journalism packaged with a focus of brevity but unwavering in quality. There will always be a place for the more verbose David Broder-ish or William F. Buckley-esque essays, which drill deep and examine the issues of our times, but our current day-to-day media condition stresses brevity and as Jim VandeHei believes it is a brevity rooted in a simple, relatable vocabulary with a firm hand on the throttle which controls both word count and the clock.

It was an enjoyable conversation. I find VandeHei's evolution from the ornate and almost stentorian newsrooms of the late 20th century to the work-from-home, shorts and sandals, "How Ya' Doin" approach to 2020s journalism quite interesting. I also find his respect for using language as a tool of effective everyday professional and personal brevity refreshing. It turns out you can teach an old dog (oops, sorry, Jim, a middle-aged dog) new tricks.

By the way, I must have kept the Kalegi Word Count within the acceptable range. As I thanked him for his time, Jim never brought it up.

Whew.

14

Doris Kearns Goodwin

Author, Presidential Historian, Winner of the Pulitzer Prize

I've spent 50 years of my life waking up with dead presidents.

***

I first became aware of Doris Kearns Goodwin when I saw her as one of the erudite talking heads in Ken Burns' groundbreaking documentary *Baseball.* She grew up in Rockville Center, New York, a fervent Brooklyn Dodgers fan who, for a while, lost her affinity for the game after Walter O'Malley ripped her Dodgers out by their Brooklyn roots and transplanted them three thousand miles away in Los Angeles. Years later, after settling in New England, she developed a similar love for the Boston Red Sox. I then began enjoying Doris' appearances with Tim Russert on NBC's *Meet the Press* and her conversations with Don Imus. She's always been able to analyze contemporary issues through an informed prism of historical perspective.

My initial conversation with Doris took place smack dab in the middle of the Trump administration, an unsettled time in American politics, to say the very least. It was October of 2019, and we were only a couple of months away from first hearing about COVID-19 and less than six months away from the world shutting down and, in many ways, changing forever. We discussed how presidents handle turbulent times. Doris and I had no idea how turbulent our times were about to become.

It was great to say hello to Doris Kearns Goodwin.

I began by citing Shakespeare. As Antonio proclaims in *The Tempest*: "What's past is prologue." If this is true, American history can be considered a primer to contemporary times. Considering that current era of turbulence, I asked Doris if it's been difficult not to draw comparisons to current times in her more recent writings. She immediately brought up "her guys."

I've just been thinking about the turbulent times that my guys lived through: Abraham Lincoln, the two Roosevelts, and Lyndon Johnson. I do think, however, what it can teach us about today is that when we've been through these really tough times before, we can get some solace in knowing that we lived through even tougher times and we got through them. But the reason we got through them was because there was a combination of the right leader at the right time and people who were active.

I then wondered if there's any direct correlation between citizen activism and the perceived success of an American president. Doris cited the anti-slavery movement as being critical of what Lincoln was able to accomplish. She then mentioned how the people established the progressive movement in the cities and states before Teddy Roosevelt and FDR, and the Civil Rights Movement was firmly in place before Lyndon Johnson.

So, I think it tells us as citizens today that if we feel we're in a troubled time, citizen activism and taking charge of our problems is really a key and not just simply waiting around for the right leader to come through.

I couldn't resist the reference Doris made a bit earlier about "her guys." I asked why Lincoln, the two Roosevelts, and LBJ comprise her personal Mount Rushmore. She said it's simply because she knows them the best: *I've spent 50 years of life waking up with dead presidents and wanting to think about them when I go to bed at night.* Doris went on to say that she realized some of them had been better leaders than the others. Lyndon Johnson had his problems with Vietnam, which she believes cut his legacy in two. But overall, she stressed how they each individually became leaders, handled adversity, and dealt with crises. This made me think about leadership itself. Is it true that leadership is something that can be created and cultivated through one's contemporary experience, or is it a true intrinsic value that must already be there?

Oh Ed, it's a great question. It's one of the ones we used to debate when we were in graduate school at Harvard. I think some qualities could be intrinsic or born within, like Lincoln's was profoundly empathetic from the time he was young. He had a gift for language. Teddy Roosevelt had a photographic memory. FDR had this wonderful optimistic temperament he was born with, and LBJ just had unbounded energy. But I think mostly leaders are made, not born. Teddy Roosevelt wrote an essay once where he said there's two kinds of success in the world. The first comes if you have a talent that someone else, no matter how hard they emulate, will be unlikely to match, a great poet perhaps, or a great runner. But he said most people's success comes when they develop ordinary qualities to an extraordinary degree through hard, sustained work. He might have added through the ability to grow by having the humility to acknowledge your errors and learn from your mistakes, taking responsibility for failures, and getting through tough times. So, I think absolutely, yes, leadership can be learned as you go along and as you continue to grow.

I was immediately intrigued when Doris mentioned humility, which I believe is an extremely underrated character trait. My next question centered on the assumption that, for anyone in any position of power, you need to be able to stop and look inside yourself, not as a leader per se, but look at yourself as the human being who's doing the leading. I asked Doris to take me deeper into the concept that humility is key to the ability to lead others.

I think it's absolutely central. You know, I think we sometimes define humility wrong as humbleness, and what it really means, though, is exactly what you are saying. The self-reflection to look at oneself at a certain point of time and ask where could I have done better? Where did I go wrong? What can I do to make myself a better leader? That means that you realize you're not THE person in charge just because you're at the top. Maybe it doesn't mean you can't grow or you can't go back downward. Lincoln learned that early on through failure. I think he lost so many elections and he learned how to keep going. Teddy was pretty arrogant when he first got into the state legislature. They said he still wanted to be the center of attention, that he wanted to be the baby at the baptism, the bride at the wedding, and the corpse at the funeral. Teddy started yelling and pounding his desk and after a while people got tired of him and he realized he had gotten a swollen head and later said he learned from that experience. So I think it's that way of self-reflection that is absolutely key.

Leadership is a concept that has been often discussed and debated but usually in its most basic definition. It's not something where you can simply flip Webster's open and find a true one-size-fits-all definition. It's not an off-the-rack proposition. Everyone brings their own personality and their own life experience to their ability to lead. One's leadership acumen is as unique as one's fingerprint. I asked Doris if I was wrong in thinking that.

No, that's absolutely right. Nobody possesses all the strengths that someone might demand if they came up with a leadership index. The key question which is rarely asked is: does the person have the strengths needed in the particular moment, the strengths that match the current situation?

Doris cited FDR's "optimistic temperament" and his contagious ability to allow people to believe in his own confidence so that they themselves felt confident. The fireside chats were critical in bringing America through the Depression and later through World War II. Lincoln had the humility to surround himself with people who were better known, better educated, and more celebrated than he. LBJ was willing to risk everything for civil rights, which somehow became the central point of what he wanted to be remembered for and made a difference in who he was.

I keyed in on her FDR reference. "Doris, I think of Roosevelt leading a nation for an incredibly long time, a tremendously difficult period while facing physical limitations in a world which at the time was very unforgiving and quite Neanderthal in its thinking about people with challenges. Do we underestimate how much his personal challenges helped shape FDR as president?"

There's no question, said Doris. *Because of becoming paralyzed from the waist down when he was still in his thirties he too, as I say, learned humility. He used to have to crawl around the carpet floor for hours to strengthen his upper body. FDR said you learned humility this way. He also learned how to connect to people to whom fate had also dealt an unkind hand. FDR had come from such a privileged background and coming through that personal crisis, the paralysis that he himself had underwent when the country was in its own paralysis in 1930, '31, and '32, when he's running for and when he becomes president, there's something that transforms itself and transforms within himself that enables him to bring people to a greater sense of purpose.*

Doris Kearns Goodwin has the unique ability to describe history and define it from a perspective that is quite contemporary. It's quite a talent to, in a literary sense, bring to life people, places, and times that are long gone and stream them through a prism of relevance. I love the fact that she has "her guys," these four American presidents whom she uses as a fulcrum for her exploration of history. Lincoln, both Roosevelts, and Lyndon Johnson each dealt with major issues, troubles, and turbulence that were unique to their times. Were they all successful? In some cases, most definitely. In the case of Johnson, the victory of Civil Rights was tempered by a Vietnam situation that escalated and worsened on his watch and the unrest at home, which comprised 1968 and guided LBJ to not run for re-election.

Considering where our country stood in October of 2019, in the middle of a presidency that was becoming increasingly divisive by the day, I thought Doris was the perfect person to bring historical guidance to my audience. That moment in our history was the right time for such a conversation. I found it extremely interesting that she talked about presidents who handled difficult times by looking inside themselves and discovering traits that provided insight and strength. I believe Doris was looking to provide hope, and hope is always a good thing. Quite simply, you can't trigger progress without it.

As we know, only a few months later, the world changed. We endured a years-long global pandemic that claimed way too many of our loved ones, including my father. After the murder of George Floyd at the hands of police, we witnessed a racial reckoning that ignited a true and meaningful conversation, unlike previous ones, which were merely peripheral in nature. We also started talking about what freedom and justice truly mean in our current American society.

Over the past few years, we've seen and suffered great sorrow but also have sown the seeds of tremendous hope. We've proven once again that turbulence can lead to renewal. What I enjoyed most about my conversation with Doris is that she demonstrated my long-held conviction about historians: they provide a clear understanding of where we've been as we navigate where we are now and where we are headed into the future.

Remember, never forget what Antonio said: "What's past is prologue."

15

Dean Koontz

Author, International Bestselling Master of Suspense

My father was diagnosed first as borderline schizophrenic with tendencies to violence complicated by alcoholism, and then later diagnosed as sociopathic. That's why I think I'm drawn to bad guys and sociopaths because I understand how their minds work.

***

I love talking with authors, especially fiction authors. These are people with incredibly fertile imaginations, people who give literary birth to characters and build the worlds in which these characters live. They are true artists whose palettes and canvases exist in their minds. Their stories provide enjoyment, evoke emotion, and stir thought. Their stories live forever.

Every author I've ever spoken with is unique. No two are alike, and each has an interesting personal story. Those personal stories create the framework and foundation for the literary gifts they bestow on the world.

I entered the studio and sat at the mic, ready to engage one of the world's most creative minds, a mind responsible for creating over a hundred novels, many novellas, and short stories. It has been reported that his works have sold over 450 million copies. He is the true master of suspense.

It was great to say hello to Dean Koontz.

Koontz is one of those authors that other writers hold in high regard. Actually, when I found out Dean was booked on my show, another author who wrote suspense blended with a delicious dash of horror and satire exclaimed: "You have Dean Koontz coming on your show?!?" First of all, she said this in such a high tone of excitement. Her vocal variety of harmonics was only truly discernable by goats. Secondly, it was said with the same giddiness and adulation as displayed by a tearful teenage girl swooning at the sight of The Beatles at Shea Stadium back in 1965. Obviously, Dean Koontz is quite an icon within the writing community.

When speaking with an author of this caliber and level of achievement, there is a trap of overthinking the conversation, of trying to come up with a perfect yet overly ethereal question with which to begin. I decided to forego the Rolls Royce and instead jump in the Toyota with a relatively basic question I've asked other writers.

"Dean, the characters in your stories are so well developed, they have so much texture. I'm wondering, for you, does the story drive the characters or do the characters drive the story?"

Ed, when I was young and stupid, which wasn't that many years ago as I stayed stupid a long time, I thought that story was it, and in fact, pretty quickly over this career, I came to the conclusion that characters were more important. That you could have the greatest story in the world, but if you didn't care about the characters, you wouldn't care about the story that much, either. And ideally, the story is just as gripping as the characters. But for many years now, the characters have come first to me. I get the story premise. I don't have an outline. I don't know where it's going. But if I have a character or two that I think within a few pages you're going to be fasci-

nated with, then I know the story is going to work, and the characters will take it places that I never would have taken it in an outline.

Dean continued with a wonderfully introspective dissertation on the importance of character and how he believes the characters he creates are living and breathing beings who seemingly display will, choice, and sometimes even control.

You just let them develop, and they'll suddenly start doing things, and I'll stop writing and say, "No, no, no, that's terrible. You can't do that! That's the wrong way to do it, that's the wrong way to go." And I've learned, let the character do it, and you'll be surprised where this is going to lead. It's very mysterious. But one of the great things about this work, about trying to get it done, is to just let the characters guide you.

"Dean, at what point does a character become real enough for you to write about him or her? How long does that character have to live inside your mind and inside your soul before that character appears on paper?"

Generally, it's pretty quick. I have a drawer full of novel ideas; when an idea comes to me, I think, "Ooh, that's good." I write it down and put it in the drawer. But I never go back to that drawer because there's always some new and better idea coming along that captivates me. And when it captivates you, you think, "I gotta get that written now." So I sit down, and I start, and I get a character. If that character, within 10 to 20 pages, isn't enough for me to want to know more and more and more, then it's the wrong character. And maybe it's a story that isn't gonna work either. So, if they're good, they come alive pretty quickly, and once you've got a handle on them, they kind of grow, just like a relationship with a real person grows in your life.

I then wondered about the other end of essentially the same question. After a novel is complete and he's taken a character through their journey, considering that character is of him and from him, how long does a character remain in Dean's consciousness after he's finished writing a book? Dean paused, admitted he does think about his characters after the creative deed is done, and explained his process.

That's why, in the end, I always want to give the reader a fairly full sense of where a character is going after a particular story so that you feel a little finished. It's like they're still going on out there in life. But sometimes a character comes to you like Odd Thomas came to me, and one book isn't enough. I could have written probably 30 books with Odd Thomas, but I wrote eight because there was a promise made to him in Book One that I felt I was obligated to keep to him, that I was going to end up tormenting him too much to draw his story out too far. Ed, I got lots of requests to write more about him. But no, his story took eight books to tell, and he needed a conclusion. He needed the promise that was made in the beginning of the series that could be delivered to him.

At this point, I felt as if our conversation had just turned surreal. Dean became quite immersed in the answer to my original question. He talked about his character of Odd Thomas as someone who was quite real, quite tangible, and someone to whom he owed the obligation of fulfilling a special promise. His care for Odd Thomas was surprisingly emotional and palpable. He sounded incredibly protective and paternal at this point, and I must admit I was curiously fascinated by his tone.

This was a good point to begin examining Dean Koontz's effect on other writers. I thought of the author I mentioned earlier who went totally giddy when I told her one of her literary idols was scheduled to chat with little old me.

"Dean, what is it like when someone tells you that you were their inspiration to write or when you hear yourself and your works quoted back to you?"

It's strange when that starts to happen. You get mail from readers, and some of them become writers, and they will tell you that you've inspired them and that you were the first writer that they read and got hooked on. At first, I took it with a grain of salt because I just didn't quite believe it. But as it began to happen more and more, I began to think back to the writers that had a very profound effect on me. One of them was John D. McDonald, a writer who showed me that character was just as important as anything. When I first found McDonald's books, I read 34 novels in 30 days.

"Wow," I said, trying to digest the idea of reading 34 books in 30 days.

I did nothing else. It had a very profound effect on me, and certain other writers have had that same effect. It's the nicest, sweetest thing somebody can say to you, and I finally got the idea that, gee, maybe this is true. Ed, it's kind of daunting to think that this happens, right? But books have power. They have a lot of power and I know that because they changed my life.

I appreciated Dean's use of the word "power." The written word has power, unlike any other form of communication. When you are an author, as someone who reads your words, story, and characters, that reader creates their own internal scenescape, which embraces and breathes life into a uniquely personal universe of *your* words. That's the bridge to the visual. And so, the words, if they are powerful, can conjure up a plethora of powerful images for the reader that remain with them. Many last forever.

Dean then interjected his thoughts about the different types of writers that exist.

There are two kinds of, well, there's probably more than two kinds, Ed, but there's two fundamental types of writers. There's the kind who like having written, they like what comes after they deliver the book. They like the book signings and the publicity and all of that, but they're not really keen on the daily grind of the writing. I like the writing part better than what comes afterward. I enjoy fading away into the fictional world in a way that is kind of marvelous.

At this point, Dean whetted my appetite, and I became intrigued by his writing process. "When do you write? Do you schedule a time to write? What inspires you to write?"

I get up at about 5:00. I walk the dog and feed the dog, and then we cuddle. I'm here at about 6:30, and I work straight through until dinner. And I do that six days a week for the most part. I love those kinds of sessions. I've never had writer's block. And I always say to young writers all writer's block is the same thing. It's self-doubt. I have more self-doubt than any writer I've ever met, but you have to power through it. The way I power through it is I rewrite every page over and over until it's very smooth. Then I move to the next page, and then the self-doubt comes back again. But you get through the book anyway, and it becomes your life. But it's not a bad life. Even if you don't become a bestseller and simply make an okay living at it, it's still a grand way to make a living.

"I would imagine, Dean, it's also a great way to have an inner communication with yourself as you develop these ideas and you develop these characters by completely fleshing them out and giving them life. That must be an amazing feeling to be able to do that. Are you writing longhand, or are you typing?"

Dean told me he's written one thing longhand during his long career. He was writing a book using a keyboard, and a line came into his head: My name is Odd Thomas, *and I lead an unusual life.* He knew it had nothing to do with what he was currently writing, so he turned to a legal pad and wrote it our longhand. He couldn't stop and wrote the entire first chapter of *Odd Thomas* longhand. Dean said it was a rare occurrence and quite a mystery to him where it came from. But mostly, he's at his computer pecking away on the keyboard because of the convenience it provides, especially with revisions.

"Dean, technology is a very important part of your writing. Why is tech so important for you in the creation of your work?"

Well, at some point, you realize technology is reshaping the world so fast that, as a writer, you need to touch upon it in stories. In fact, that gave me the whole Jane Hawk series, which were books about some really bad high technology and how you can remain free in a world where there's universal surveillance.

Obviously, Dean has an incredibly fertile imagination that evolves with the times and the world around him. But I began to wonder, overall, if Dean ever encountered any misconceptions about authors who write suspense and horror.

Sometimes, when my wife's been with me at a book signing, people will say to her, "I don't know if I could be married to him, he's so scary." The stereotype is that if you can imagine these things and invent them, then there must be something wrong with you. And certainly, if you talk to my wife long enough, you'll find out there are things wrong with me. But it's not that I'm particularly scary. In spite of the darkness in a lot of my books, there's also hope because I am basically the biggest optimist you'll ever meet.

That's what I wanted to discover, the true Koontz. I then was a bit surprised because, without prodding or any specific curiosity shown by me, Dean opened up and talked about his upbringing in a very personal way and how that has shaped not only who he is today but why some of the characters he creates are the way they are.

I came out of poverty, from a family that was tremendously dysfunctional because my dad was a violent alcoholic. When I was eight, I started getting interested in books and writing, and it was largely because books early on became an escape from an untenable house. They gave me hope and showed me different lives, ones other than ours, and that was important. Later in life, when I had to take over support of my father for the last 14 years of his life, and we moved him to California, he ended up in trouble in a number of ways. He ended up in the psych ward at one point. My father was diagnosed first as borderline schizophrenic with tendencies to violence complicated by alcoholism, and then later diagnosed as sociopathic. That's why I think I'm drawn to bad guys and sociopaths because I understand how their minds work. They're brilliant at faking human emotion. So, in a backhanded sort of way, a big part of my career came from how I was raised and my ability to understand certain things, things I don't know that I would've understood if I hadn't lived through them in that fashion.

"Dean, if you weren't a writer, what do you think your vocation in life would've been?"

I was a teacher for a while. I worked in a poverty program as a tutor for underprivileged children. That was one year, and then a year and a half in public school as a teacher. But I got so fed up with the bureaucracy of education, where most of the money for education doesn't seem to actually go into educating anyone. I don't think I could've ever lasted terribly long as a teacher, although I loved the kids and I loved the teaching, but it was that bureaucracy that stifles you. Other than that, I don't know what I could have done. I look at it now and think I'd probably have a life in crime, but I wouldn't have been very good at it. So, thank God that option wasn't one I had to take.

I laughed at that sudden and dry slice of Dean's humor. I told him I'd much rather see his picture on the back of one of his books instead of on the wall in a post office somewhere. I then moved toward my final question, but I decided I would put a bit of a spin on it.

"Dean, what is the one interview question no one has ever asked you but you wish they would?

Gee, I've been asked so many questions. You know, Ed, I do wish sometimes people would understand I dedicate a lot of books to my wife. I wish there was some way for people to understand how important it is in a career that's been this prolific for this long, that you have somebody in your life who loves you and that you love, and that relationship remains strong no matter what. She's just an absolutely great lady, and anybody who could stay married to me for over half a century has to be somebody exceptional.

What a wonderful and unexpected love letter from Dean to his wife. Considering this is a man who is known for a specific genre of writing that is not necessarily the makings of a Hallmark card, this was a side of Dean I didn't think would reveal itself in our conversation. But I'm very glad it did. Here was an author, the master of suspense, who delved into horror, fantasy, science fiction, and mystery, and he concluded a great conversation about the power of love. I sensed from Dean that nothing could change or alter his feelings for that one special person in his life, not even the most twisted, unexpected, and macabre story he could concoct in his mind. Love endures no matter what happens, be it wonderful, mundane, or even horribly sudden and tragic.

Love is eternal. Even the goats who decode the vocal variety of unique harmonics know that.

16

Richard Lewis

Actor, Comedian, Author

When I got on stage, I felt so lost, and I said the only way I could feel validated would be to talk about how miserable I feel. If I got laughs, then I knew I wasn't crazy and that other people felt the same way.

***

He was a comedian who developed a very unique act because he was a very unique individual. Over 50 years in the business, with a definite imprint made upon stand-up, sitcoms with Don Rickles and then with Jamie Lee Curtis, followed by a long recurring run on *Curb Your Enthusiasm.* He reintroduced himself to each rising generation. Yet his comedy and his personality remained consistent. That's a successful career in show business by any measure.

It was great to say hello to Richard Lewis.

In April of 2023, Richard announced that he was suffering from Parkinson's Disease; his number of public appearances had been shrinking for a while, yet he was still making occasional appearances on *Curb* with his long-time friend, Larry David. Richard handled this new phase of his life with grace and class. On February 27, 2024, Richard passed away.

I had the pleasure of first having Richard on my show a few years prior to his Parkinson's announcement, and it was vintage Richard Lewis. His personality and quintessential tone made the three-thousand-mile geographic distance disappear. It was a fun conversation with a guy who was as funny as he was interesting. Off we went.

"Comedy Central considers my next guest one of the top 50 standup comedians of all time," I began. "*GQ Magazine* called him one of the 20th century's most influential humorists, and it sure as hell ups my street cred by having him on the show. I've wanted to have him on since the first minute I got this show. It is great to say hello to Richard Lewis."

Ed, it's about time, said Richard. *It's The Weekend, and I need you more than you need me.*

"I don't think so, Richard."

No, no, I do. You're syndicated, you're a big shot; I'm just an old man with bad posture, been doing this for over 45 years, and a recovering drug addict. I need you, Ed.

"Wow, that warms my heart. What a way to start an interview."

Well, I meant every word of it. Are we done yet?

It was the best start to any conversation I've ever had on the show. Richard was always pitch-perfect. He was someone who has always borne his soul in his comedy so, since he supposedly needed me more than I needed him, I dug right in.

"Richard, one of the things I've always enjoyed about you is how you're willing to look inside yourself for material instead of just looking at the world around you. How difficult is that to do? I mean, you've been in the business well over 40 years now, but when you made that decision that you yourself were going to be the basis of a lot of your material, how difficult was that at first to explore and actually do?"

Well, Ed, listen, there've been some great observational comedians, but frankly, my father died before I was a performer. My sister eloped when I was 12. My brother was already out of the house. My mother had a lot of problems, the poor thing, so I had really no family to speak of. When I got on stage, I felt so lost, and I said the only way I could feel validated would be to talk about how miserable I feel. If I got laughs, then I knew I wasn't crazy and that other people felt the same way. So, I like to sort of unravel the onion when I'm on stage. I have no idea what I'm gonna say when I go on stage. I have thousands of hours of material on my computer, and I look at it, but, you know, at about, you know, maybe 2, 3, 4 hours of new material, but I can hardly remember it.

Right there, Richard hit the comedy nail on the head. He was one of the first truly conversational comics, a steady stream of consciousness that takes the audience deep within the Lewis psyche and deeper into his personal comedic DNA. Richard then told me more about why his comedy is the way it is and what he's always tried to steer clear of.

I never wanted to judge, to say, "Hey, do you ever notice when you go to a store?" That kind of humor is good for people, and they laugh. There's nothing wrong with it, but that would've been meaningless for me. That would've been what happened to me. I was always judged and told. So, I'd rather just say, "Here's how I feel." That's more important, and it is a thin line between narcissism and comedy. But, if people couldn't laugh at how I was feeling, then I just would've quit. Apparently, for 45 years, they're still hanging in. So, I'm grateful.

Richard got sober in 1994. I wondered how that changed his comedy.

I once made a joke that I have so much clarity now that I despise myself even more. It was a good little line, but the truth of the matter is, when I was doing well, I was a functioning alcoholic, and I don't like that phrase because there were a lot of things I could have done, which I didn't, because my life was sort of outta control. But I managed to pull off a TV series and concerts and big shows and do it without being hammered. But that didn't make me a good guy. It just made me lucky, you know? But when I finally, uh, when I finally got sober, I was clear-headed enough to realize that I wasn't just the victim.

Richard's sobriety provided him with both perspective and clarity.

That's why I came up with things from hell. I was always blaming everybody, and I still do to some degree, but I also realize that I have a part in the equation, too. So, it's given me twice as much material because it's like, not only was my mother or my girlfriend from hell, look, my mother tried. I don't like saying that about my mom, but you know, the truth is she had problems. But rather than say mother from hell or girlfriend from hell, I can say I was a boyfriend and a son from hell. And I have a whole load of material about myself because I was no cool guy either. So, it just made it easier for me to put myself down on stage, which I liked.

Speaking of the "whomever" from hell, there is an episode of *Curb* where Richard is trying to get credit in *Bartlett's* for the infamous quotation. For the purpose of conversation, it was an opportunity to set the record straight.

"Richard, are you really the guy who invented the phrase *the _______ from hell?*"

It's in the Yale Book of Quotations. *See, you know, it's funny because I've been doing it since the early '70s, and I remember doing it on* Letterman *all the time. And David would stop me and say, "I know you came from a party from hell." I did popularize the phrase and I remember trying to have my lawyer try to get it into* Bartletts. *And the editor says, "Nah, it wasn't Richard." I said, "What do you mean it wasn't Richard?" I'd been doing it for 30 years and it was never popularized before that. And he said, "My nieces just came back from college and they said they had a semester from hell." I told him they were probably watching me on* Letterman!

We then finished our time together talking NBA basketball for a few minutes. I'm a fan of the Brooklyn Nets, primarily because they were once the New Jersey Nets that, from 1977 until 1981, played their home games at Rutgers. Thus, I had an NBA team literally two and a half miles from my childhood home. Richard, on the other hand, was a lifelong fan of the New York Knicks, who, when we spoke, were having yet another underachieving season. Over the years, Richard was often seen sitting in Celebrity Row at Madison Square Garden. He was a true fan who knew his team and knew the game. He was never a bandwagon jumper, nor was he a celebrity going to Knicks games simply for the front-row seat and to have his face shown on the video board. He was a legit Knicks fan.

Richard Lewis was one of the more down-to-earth celebrities I've had on the show. I was a bit surprised at how easy and approachable he was: hilarious and incredibly introspective during the same conversation. At this point in his life journey, he was very comfortable in his own skin, and he maintained that wonderful gift of humor. His was a personal treasure chest filled with perspective.

It's a lesson for us all. Rest well, Richard.

17

Robert Klein

Comedian, Singer, Actor

Jerry Seinfeld says I was The Beatles of comedy to him.

***

The first time I saw Robert Klein perform was in the early spring of 1986 at the Forum Theater in my current hometown of Metuchen, New Jersey. As I sat centerstage in the fifth row along with a girlfriend from my high school and college years, I carefully watched a master craftsman at work, creating a distinct vibe with the audience as he maintained a unique cadence with his material. Here was a guy in the prime of his career, as extremely funny and topical as he was when America first met him on *The Ed Sullivan Show* back in 1970. As someone who has always performed from the perspective of "Be Funny First," it was an evening that left quite an impression.

Fast forward nine years: it's 1995, and I'm now married and living in Metuchen, to a different girl, by the way, if you're keeping score. It was a Friday morning in October, and later that evening, Robert Klein was returning to the Forum Theater, this time to tape his 6th HBO Comedy Special: *It All Started Here.* Unfortunately for me, I wouldn't be in the audience that night. My wife and I had already booked a long weekend at Walt Disney World and were flying down that afternoon. That morning, though, as I was returning home after picking up our dry cleaning, I was sitting at a traffic light downtown, and there across the street was Robert Klein. He was hours away from taping an HBO special, but there he was, sitting at a table outside of Lucca's Coffee Shop, sipping from a Styrofoam cup and reading a newspaper. There was quite an urge to park my 1991 Dodge Shadow, go over, and say hello, but there was a stronger urge not to miss our flight, which was leaving from Newark only three hours later.

"Damn," I thought to myself, "I missed the only chance I'll ever have to chat with Robert Klein." Fast forward many years later, and there I was, sitting in the studio along with the audio producer, waiting for Robert to call my nationally syndicated radio show.

It was great to say hello to Robert Klein.

My conversation with Robert dovetailed with the release of the sometimes hilarious, often poignant, and always entertaining documentary: *Robert Klein Still Can't Stop His Leg.* After seeing the film and learning of the impact Robert had on the generation of comics that followed him, I immediately had my introduction for Robert set in my mind.

"Welcome back, I'm Ed Kalegi. It's been written and it may very well be true that without my next guest, modern standup comedy simply may not exist. It is great to say hello to Robert Klein. Robert, welcome to the show."

Hey, thanks, Ed. Wow, Jesus, that's quite an introduction.

I mentioned to Robert right off the bat how, at least to me, he is the comic I hear in so many other comics. I can literally hear the DNA, and the one who always presented the most striking Klein-like lineage to me is Jerry Seinfeld. Both are masters of the everyday educated observational genre and work clean. Over the years, as comedy went from PG to R to NC-17 and even X in a couple of cases, both Klein and Seinfeld not only survived but thrived by working creatively with their minds, they never leaned on the shock value of overly scatological humor. Ironically, both found tremendous success outside of stand-up: Klein in both film and television as well as on the Broadway stage, and Seinfeld in, perhaps, the best sitcom ever seen on American TV.

Jerry Seinfeld says I was The Beatles of comedy to him, and I've heard similar things from Jay Leno, Jon Stewart, Bill Maher, and Billy Crystal. I mean to hear all this, it's like being Huckleberry Finn at my own funeral as I'm listening to all this, you know?

What makes *Robert Klein Still Can't Stop His Leg* such a compelling watch is that you have several giants of comedy showering praise upon Klein, which in no way is manufactured. It's legitimate, it's tangible, and it's real.

"It is quite amazing that, for you, it is like hearing a eulogy while you're still here and still working, but what I took from what I saw is this is like a roast without the nastiness; they are simply telling you what you mean to them."

Exactly right, it is like hearing your own eulogy. It's also a very funny movie and was three years in the making. This was bigger than Ben-Hur, *except there is no chase scene with the chariots. It shows me my current life. I live mostly in the Hudson River Valley here, across the river from you.*

I then asked Robert to tell me more about his current life.

Well, I live mostly in the Hudson River Valley, but I also have a little apartment in New York. I've been divorced for 29 years, which was not pretty, but I go to the supermarket and feel the fruit and do my shopping. I'm still working, and I'm still alive. I'm exhausted; I just came back from Florida, where I did five shows. But I do have a workout regimen. I'm still in pretty good shape. I went to a college reunion with about 12 guys last year. I couldn't believe it; these guys were falling apart.

Robert never fell apart as, for decades, he worked at a frenetic pace. It could be said that Robert Klein is the most versatile of all the standup comics in the modern entertainment age. His career actually dates back to 1957, when he made an appearance along with his singing group, The Teen Tones, on *Ted Mack's Amateur Hour.* Some years later, a long career began, which eventually took Robert through Broadway, where he won a Tony Award in 1979 for his work in the musical comedy *They're Playing Our Song,* and also out to Hollywood, where he has enjoyed a legitimate career as both a comedic and dramatic actor. Scrolling through his IMDB is a leading cause of carpal tunnel syndrome. Other comics have tried to stretch their personalities and careers onto the stage and on film and TV, but Klein has maintained a consistency of performance and frequency of work, which other guys simply could not match.

Robert Klein was also a pioneer of long-form cable television comedy specials. In 1975, he did the first HBO Comedy Special. I wondered if he knew, back then, how groundbreaking it truly was. "That HBO special back in '75 changed everything on so many different levels. It was the first time you got your act into a home, on TV, uncensored. Plus, there was no time restriction. You weren't boxed into a seven-minute set on the Carson show just before Angie Dickinson came out to flirt with Johnny."

You got it, Ed.

"Did you know back then, Robert, how this new way of doing comedy was going to change the entire landscape of comedy?"

No, not at all. It was the idea of a guy named Harlan Kleiman, who was a vice president at HBO at the time and went on to become an investment banker on the West Coast. At the time, HBO was very small with only half a million subscribers in 1975. It was a tiny operation with only a couple of dozen people in an office and now it's the biggest money maker in that company, I think. And it's entirely due to me.

I laughed as Robert delivered that last line in quintessential Klein style, with both irony and hubris on full display.

But seriously, Ed, it was a magnificent change. I don't work particularly blue, but of course, we're all adults, and we should be able to use some language. I was so restricted in those times when I started; there were three networks and every word you said on The Tonight Show *or on* Cavett, *or whatever the thing was, they really wanted to know ahead of time. You couldn't suggest, you couldn't say lots of things. Ed, a minute ago, you hit it right on the nose. I could do a complete show. I was doing a lot of college concerts, and that's where the genius came in. This was uninterrupted, paid TV, say what you want TV, you know? Of course, now it's gone so far the other way that every second word is a profanity, which I have no objection to, personally, but I just don't watch it if I don't like it.*

Robert then became quite introspective and seemed to look to put both his career and his life in perspective.

When I think about my life and my career, I don't have any regrets, really. I mean, what could I wish for if I were thinking of how it would turn out? I did it on my terms. I wasn't the biggest comedian of all time, or the biggest movie star, but, you know, I've done everything. And one of the things that kept me interested and working was versatility. You know, I've been in over 40 feature films, hundreds of television shows, five or six Broadway shows, a book, and about four albums. I don't know what else there is to do. I'm too old for Hamlet.

"Wait a minute," I jumped in, "if there's a Hudson Valley performance of *Hamlet*, they can call you and you'll give it a shot, right?"

I'm old enough for Polonius, Ed. But he was a schmuck.

And with that pitch-perfect ending, it was time to say goodbye to Robert.

"This has been quite a bucket list moment for me. Robert Klein, thank you so much for joining me here on *The Weekend.*"

Thanks, Ed, I've enjoyed this very much.

I then did my customary "stay with us, more to come" lockout to end the recorded radio segment. The audio producer at the radio station where I recorded the interview still had Robert on the line. Again, I took the opportunity to thank Robert for his time and the great conversation. I told him of the deep impression he made on me when I sat fifth-row center at the Forum in the spring of '86. I also mentioned how I regretted passing up the opportunity to stop and say Hi nine years later that Friday morning on Main Street in Metuchen.

Well, wasn't this better than accosting me on the street? said Robert in an astonished chuckle.

Yeah, it sure was.

18

Dick Cavett

Television Talk Show Host

Do you have to go through your life saying, "Kalegi, spelled the usual way?"

***

This one is special. I've often talked about my affinity for Dick Cavett, his talent, his wit, his intelligence, and his place in television history. He, for me, will always be the gold standard. No one comes close. Only three weeks after the show's debut, I had the chance to have a conversation with the person I watched as a kid and said, "I wanna do THAT one day." And I did.

It was a cloudy but hot and sticky August morning as I started the car and began the long ride to the radio station. In the show's early years, we recorded each week at a station 53 miles from home as the crow files. Since I'm not a crow, nor can fly, that 53-mile drive stretched and strained its way to about 60 miles through some very winding roads across New Jersey. There was a benefit, though. The long ride always gave me a chance to think about the people I would be chatting with that day for the upcoming weekend's show. On this day, only one guest was scheduled, so there was only one to think about. It was Dick Cavett.

As I drove, I felt several emotions that seemed to change as often as the traffic lights that regulated my long suburban ride that summer morning. First, yeah, I was a bit nervous, but who wouldn't be? I mean, c'mon, this is Dick Cavett we're talking about here. Second, I was a bit nostalgic. I remembered seeing Cavett when I was a kid back in the '70s in my bedroom on my portable Sony black and white TV with a five-inch screen. As I drove to the studio that day, I could see that image of Cavett controlled by the snowy and wiggly picture inherent to the sketchy reception of the aforementioned tiny TV. But more than anything else, I felt proud. This was the bucket list of bucket lists. Cavett was the perfect person to engage in conversation, and I saw this as a huge opportunity. Not very long before, as I sat in that dreary little dusty studio doing inane and repetitive traffic reports, I yearned for this. I craved a show that would give me a platform to talk and discuss and explore and communicate. Cavett was the pinnacle, the model of all of that for me, and I lived for a day when I would be able to welcome him to *my* show. Well, that day was this day.

It was great to say hello to Dick Cavett.

I needed to frame our conversation. When we spoke, it coincided with the debut of the PBS Documentary *Dick Cavett's Watergate.* Since it was August, that also meant we were approaching yet another anniversary of the resignation of President Richard Nixon. The Watergate period is when I first learned about and first enjoyed the work of Dick Cavett. Thus, a mélange of Cavett, Nixon, and Watergate created a most delicious appetizer for our conversation. And so, it began.

"Another August begets another anniversary of the resignation of Richard Nixon," I began. "Watergate, a seismic political scandal which created cracks through the concrete of this country's constitutional core. The result? The 37th President of the United States went from 'I'm not a crook' to 'I'm taking the next plane back to San Clemente.' My next guest played a pivotal role in how America consumed and processed the Watergate scandal. It is great to say Hello to the incomparable Dick Cavett. Dick, welcome to the show."

Hi Ed, when I was listening to you do that intro, I thought, can anything and anyone's life be that many years ago? If someone had asked me how much of my show was devoted to Watergate back in those days, I would've said probably three or four, maybe five times. But the man who knows my tapes best, a guy named Robert Bader who did the DVDs for the Cavett show, started looking through them and pulling them out, and he said, you've got a ton of stuff. Now, I never set out to do multiple Watergate shows. It was just inevitable. If Tony Randall or a jazz singer or a chef came on the show, Watergate seemed to come up all the time.

I suggested to Dick that Watergate may have been TV's first reality show. He agreed. I then mentioned how everyone each day back then needed to get their fix of what was going on with Watergate, and when 11:30 PM came, folks decided to flip over to him and see what was going on because he had the players on as Watergate was happening and as the story of it was unfolding. I commented to Dick that must have been an incredible way to cover a story.

When you've done that many shows on it, actually on all subjects, you tend to forget how many you've done on any given subject. As I watched the documentary, I don't remember having Ted Kennedy on. I do remember G. Gordon Liddy, of course, because he was such a loon and so entertaining in his strange way. The main thing I came away from Liddy's appearance was when I said: 'I know you like to teach secretaries how to kill someone instantly with a pencil.' Backstage afterwards, he showed me how and I showed him a lethal neck hold from Judo. But, yeah, there was John Mitchell and all the stars of Watergate. And Ed, you used a phrase, maybe inadvertently, that Gore Vidal uses in the show where he says: 'I had to wake up every morning, and I started to shake if I didn't get my Watergate fix every morning.' It was quite a time.

"It was the caffeine of the moment for the United States."

You couldn't stop, Ed, and it got more and more until it seemed like if you were a creative writing instructor, you'd say you're putting too many elements into this. There can't be this many crooks. There can't be this many people willing to break the law for a president with a criminal streak a yard wide. Carl Bernstein has talked about how Nixon began his Nixonism on the very first day in office. When you listen to the tapes, he's talking about who we can get and how we can get revenge on this one and is this one a Jew, you know, the usual delightful bouquet of Nixon verbalisms.

Richard Nixon remains quite the enigma in the folklore which is American political history. Here was someone who proved incredibly resilient: serving as Dwight Eisenhower's Vice President, then losing to John F. Kennedy in 1960, followed by a failed run for Governor of California in '62, then the huge bounce back by winning the presidency twice, first in '68 then by a landslide in '72. The enduring theme of Nixon's story should have been one of triumph. There was one problem, however, that being Nixon himself. The 37th President came off as someone with a great intellect and an incredible amount of potential, but as I told Cavett, Nixon carried with him a wicked streak that went right through his DNA.

I think you're right about that. It's a case of where effective psychoanalysis or psychiatry or just therapy or maybe an exercise program would've saved him. And you're absolutely right about his intellect. A friend of mine was a Time magazine reporter for the Supreme Court for several years, and he said, you waited for Nixon because he was so brilliant and his organization was genius and his arguments were unstoppable and his presentation was great. He did stuff from memory. Ed, it's a shame that this same man who had so much to give came out of the womb cackling 'I wanna be President' and managed to, despite a dreadful personality and a criminal streak. If I ever need a little lift, I go to YouTube and listen to Nixon say to his lick spittle Haldeman, um, that's an Elizabethan word I think needs reviving, "Cavett, what can we do to screw Cavett?"

"Cavett, what can we do to screw Cavett?" It is quite the example of the mean streak, of the vindictiveness, of the Nixonian picture, which became much clearer during Watergate and the years that followed. I'm glad Dick brought it up because, in my preparation, I stumbled upon a neat little factoid I wanted to present to Mr. Cavett. "The screw Cavett line: Dick, that was one of your 26 appearances on the Nixon tapes, 26 times!"

I didn't know that until two weeks ago! That was the first one that came up. Some guy's girlfriend was working on the Nixon tapes and found that first one, 'How can we screw Cavett,' and then another one, and then five more; it may even be in the thirties by now. But the weirdest thing is that Nixon ordered that about 30 Cavett shows be made for himself, maybe realizing he was gonna have a lot of free time soon or something to look at them.

I was always a huge admirer of Cavett's wit. Maybe some of it wore off on me. I decided to give it a try: "Nixon was a man ahead of his time. Dick, if he had survived into modern times, he could have just bought the Cavett show collection on DVD for himself."

I would've been happy to send it to him along with a little note that said screw you."

It's important for a brief moment to state the obvious. Nixon, at the time of his Cavett indulgence, was embroiled in great political turmoil and was still punching the clock every day in his job as the most powerful leader in the world. So, why would Nixon be consumed with seeking a vendetta against a late-night television host? Dick Cavett was just a guy from Nebraska doing a talk show with a couple of chairs, a table, and a shag rug.

The chairs weren't even mine.

But the question remained. Why did Nixon yearn to get Cavett?

I don't know. I met him twice. Once, when I was persona grata at the White House, my wife and I were invited there in our formal clothing for an evening of Shakespeare, and then, Ed, I recommend you google "Cavett Nixon New York Times" and read a column that will make you both laugh and cringe. I think the correct title is 'This Will Kill You' and it's about a chance meeting of Nixon after all of this.

Wow, that's quite the Cavett tease and a homework assignment to boot.

...and have your paper on my desk by Friday.

"Indeed, I will, Professor," I replied. "But you know Dick, there had to have been a night at least once when Nixon walked down the hallway of the residence, tugging at his tie, all worked up because he knew Johnny had Angie Dickinson on that night only to find Pat in the Presidential bedroom sheepishly watching you talk with Ehrlichman, Haig, or Liddy."

Oh, can you verify this? I love the idea, exclaimed Dick with great nostalgic relish and excitement.

Prior to our conversation, I thought I knew everything about Dick Cavett. However, there was something I learned during my research, and it had to do with how *The Dick Cavett Show* covered Watergate. On August 1, 1973, the show was taped inside the Senate Watergate Committee hearing room, and as I continued my research, I discovered a picture of Dick sitting between Howard Baker and Lowell Weicker. How does someone get that level of access? This was still a time when the worlds of entertainment and politics didn't comingle in the way they often do today. I asked Dick how the taping on Capitol Hill came to be. He said that, to this day, he still does not know. He assumes it could only have been a coup by his production staff, but Dick himself never thought it would be possible.

There were those who were very upset by it, saying, why is a cheap Vaudeville comic doing a show in the august presence of the senators and so on? But I'll tell you something, Ed, that so far could be exclusive to you because I just remembered it. Having watched the hearings from morning to night every day, I finally got down there, went into the room as an observer, and then got to meet the senators. They all came back to the room I was in, they were my heroes, and their first words to me were: "How do you manage to keep so slim?"

"Wait a minute," as I dared interrupt one of my heroes, "we're careening towards a Constitutional crisis, and THAT'S the question that comes up?"

Yup, wouldn't you think it would be at least something more pertinent?

I would think so, but then again, Dick has always kept himself in marvelously good shape, so perhaps it was an appropriate point of interest for key lawmakers that day back in the summer of '73. Anyway, the final question I asked Dick about Nixon and Watergate is one that's occupied my mind for a while. Considering that it took months and essentially years for the entire story to play out and for the process to work itself out, if there existed the ubiquitous 24-hour electronic news cycle that exists today, would the great unindicted co-conspirator, as Cavett calls him, been able to hold out for as long as he did?

I doubt it, and by the way, that's an excellent question. I think it probably would've stemmed much sooner because there's so much communication floating around now that somebody would've stumbled into something, and somebody would've made the wrong cell phone call, and somebody would've posted something that shouldn't have been.

At this point, I pivoted away from Nixon and Watergate and began a deep dive into Cavett himself. I told Dick how I've long admired the way he's been able to *not* interview people. He has conversations with people. There's a huge difference between the two.

You know, Ed, that came from my great boss, Jack Paar, who started me in show business. When I started to do my first talk show daytime on ABC that later turned into the late-night show, I got a call from Jack, and he was his usual nervous, neurotic, hilarious, wonderful, eccentric, strange self. He said, 'Hey kid, let me give you one pointer, don't do interviews.' And I thought, well, what do I do? Sing, read to the audience? He said, 'No interviews, that's Q and A.'. And that's what Jack did.

"And that's what you did. Because when you are able to relax a guest, when they know it's not gonna be question one, question two, question three, and questions they've already heard before, you have the potential to create something organic and quite magical. I was watching several of your conversations in preparation for this, and I love how you just sat back, looked at Marlon Brando, took a beat, and said, 'So do you go to the movies?'"

Dick let out a great laugh as he obviously remembered that moment with Brando and enjoyed my sardonically ironic description of it. "I mean," as I continued a bit incredulously, "who would think to ask him something like that?"

My favorite moment from that show was when I asked Brando about The Godfather, and he said, 'No, I don't talk about movies, ' *and so I said, 'Okay, how about the book* The Godfather?' *And he gave that million-dollar grin. Yeah. That seduced everybody. But what you just said earlier about conversations as opposed to Q and A interviews reminded me of probably why I got so mad at Norman Mailer on that notorious show when he got fed up and treated me as, you might say, David Frost by saying, 'Why don't you just read the next question right off the question sheet?' And that's when I said, my often misquoted, "Why don't you fold it five ways and put it where the moon doesn't shine?"'*

The Mailer incident notwithstanding, there was a feeling on the Cavett show, a tangible ambiance that was consistent and palpable to the viewer. I told Dick one of things that I admire most about him is that he always created an air of relaxed intimacy with his guests.

Hey, can I use that? I like that!

"Please do," I eagerly answered. I then immediately cited what I feel is the perfect example of this relaxed intimacy: Dick's visit with the legendary Katherine Hepburn. Turning down the sound and watching the body language within this wonderful conversation is fascinating. Watch how Hepburn's body language quickly evolves and softens. There is this woman who is this icon, and you see her, she's unassuming in almost like a coquettish slouch in her chair with her foot up on the table. It's amazing to see someone simply drop all pretense and just have a conversation as if they're standing in their backyard talking over the fence to the person who lives next to them. This is the magic of Cavett.

It's a fabulous personality display on her part, and what's interesting, and I have to see it again sometimes to believe it, is how very nervous she was at the very beginning. I could see her left cheek twitch with nerves. She was the kind of woman who, if everyone was afraid to pick up a rattlesnake, she'd make herself pick it up. She dared herself all her life, and the moment I saw that slight trembling cheek, it totally relaxed me because, as you can imagine, it gave me the feeling, oh, this woman needs my help. Then she relaxed. I don't know, people ask me what my technique is if I could describe a technique, and I never can, except I think because I identified with a guest, I knew what it felt like to sit there when I guested with Johnny or Jack or Merv or whoever.

"You knew the process. You understood what the process was."

I did, and I knew that the overriding feeling on the guest's part many times afterward was, how did you get me to tell that?

Dick then confided to me that Hepburn did some other interviews in later years with other hosts and didn't like them. She found they weren't as good. Dick told me that Hepburn admitted to him that she needed him beside her. Once again, the magic of Cavett. Dick had already mentioned Jack Paar a bit earlier during our time together. Paar was the host of *The Tonight Show* just prior to Johnny Carson and revolutionized late-night comedy in his own right. I've always observed some great and ironic similarities between Paar and Cavett: ridiculously quick wits, masters of the language, intellectually curious, and displaying social sensitivities not normally seen in their peers. I wanted to get Dick's take on Jack Paar, but first I needed some guidance. I needed him to clarify the story I had heard about how he got his job with Paar.

What part of it is obscure to you? I can clear it up, Ed.

"Okay, here goes, you're working at *Time* magazine, and one night you're watching Paar, and you think, this guy needs some better monologue material. So, you write some jokes, you put 'em in a *Time* envelope, and you take a walk over to the RCA building. You actually see Jack Paar, and you hand him the envelope with the jokes. Soon after that, he hires you. Is that the general gist, Dick?"

That's essentially it, with one correction. And this is for people who love the idea of coincidence so astonishing that they would even call it a miracle. I was a lowly copy boy at Time, *$60 a week standing at the copy desk. I glanced down at a newspaper someone happened to have left open to the right page, a gossip column. Marie Torre, a journalist colleague who went to jail for a bit for sources, and there in bold type was the name Jack Paar. I watched him every night. So, I read it, and it said that Jack worries more about his monologue than the whole show. I went home and got my old surviving Royal portable typewriter out of my Yale days and typed what sounded to me like a Jack Paar monologue. I must have written 20 jokes.*

Paar was a media personality who tended to, as they say, wear his emotions on his sleeve. He once walked off his show mid-broadcast in protest after NBC censored a rather innocuous joke about a water closet, a comment that was still perceived by network censors as a source of societal horror back in the 1960s. He returned a few weeks later. I saw actor Richard Benjamin once describe Paar as a live grenade because you never knew what would happen when Jack was on the air. But Paar was also someone who helped bring a level of sophistication that had not yet existed to conversational television. In that respect, he was the pre-Cavett. Politicians were shown to television audiences through a different prism. Intelligent, long-form conversation was embraced. New performers, such as the comedy duo of Mike Nichols and Elaine May, who focused on smart comedy for the thinking person, were given national exposure. Jack Paar gave America a brand of comedy that soothed both the brain and the funny bone. The only thing is, Paar, didn't last very long on late-night television. Since Dick worked for Paar as a *Tonight Show* writer, I figured he was the perfect person to ask why. Why didn't Paar host the show longer?

Ahh, I, who worked for Jack on The Tonight Show, *was stunned when somebody asked me not decades ago, how many years Jack was on* The Tonight Show. *I said, well, probably ten. It's five. Only five, and I person-*

ally heard him admit it's the greatest mistake he ever made. He was always in a petulant mood. I don't know how he survived living with his personality. It was the most quixotic, eccentric, neurotic, complicated, punishing, all over the place, dangerous, volatile personality I've ever been around. And that made it great for television.

"Jack Paar was a riveting watch."

Dick then mentioned Kenneth Tynan, the British critic, who once said that when he saw Jack Paar for the very first time, he realized it didn't matter who else was on the screen with him. You couldn't take your eyes off Jack, even if it were Cary Grant, because if you took your eyes off Jack, you'd be afraid you'd miss a live nervous breakdown on your television screen. I then supported Tynan's hypothesis as I told Dick that even when Paar was sitting in a chair, he had just this frenetic appearance. You could see him thinking, you could see his mind working through a situation. It was, especially for a time when television wasn't as visual as it later became, quite an odyssey to be able to watch that every night.

There's nobody who ever had anything like that to that degree. You're right. Looking at that face in a single shot. You can see things rippling and seething and bubbling and threatening to explode.

So, 1962 comes along, and Jack says goodbye. Here comes Johnny Carson. Dick stayed on as a staff writer, but how different was it? I asked Dick if he had to change what he did on a daily basis to be able to write for Johnny as opposed to Jack.

Not a great deal in the sense that if you can write for anybody, the reason you can write for them is that you can hear them in your head. Bob Hope's head writer explained that to me. He said these guys who don't make it as writers can't figure out why. It's because they word the joke wrong for Jack Benny, and they word it the same way they would for Danny Thomas or the way they would for Alan King, and they're all different. I knew how Johnny sounded from Nebraska because I would hear his radio show in Omaha when I was in high school.

I always found the Nebraska lineage shared by Cavett and Carson not just ironic but quite the study in similar presentation, humor, and even background. Both dabbled in magic early in their professional careers.

I know, said Dick, obviously surprised that I brought up the magician connection. *What else do we have in common? Well, I never married any woman whose first name began with the letter J, as Johnny did three times. But we were such good friends. When I went on with my own show, people expected me to suffer the fate Joan Rivers did with Johnny. But he would call me and chat with me about the show, and I'd call him. He was so fond of me that it almost puzzled me that we would be such good friends because his staff could never believe it because I went on his show many times. I'd go on after a Cavett show had been canceled, and Johnny would have me on the next Monday and say, "Uh, if this one doesn't work, it's, uh, Armed Forces Radio next for Richard."*

That last line made me laugh out loud, not just because of how Dick delivered it, but because the remark is quintessentially Carson. Dick then talked about a time during one appearance on the Carson show when he hadn't heard Johnny's intro as he was standing behind that many-colored curtain where one waited before walking out onto the set. Dick saw it on a monitor, but he couldn't hear it. When he got back to the hotel, he heard it when the show aired later that same evening. Carson said, "We always have a kind of fatherly feeling about Richard," and Dick told me that Carson looked a little teary as he said it. Obviously, there was a mutual affinity between Dick and Johnny that, until our conversation, was rarely talked about.

Dick Cavett is one of those personalities that, through the years, seemed to pop up in places you wouldn't expect to find him. Prior to our conversation, I did a deep dive into Dick's IMDB, and its length and diversity are quite amazing. It reaches way back to the 1950s when Dick was a background actor on an episode of *The Phil Silvers Show.* I asked Dick about it.

I do believe that it may be online somewhere.

"Really? I'd love to see that."

Oh, Ed, you really ought to see it. The episode is called "Bilko's Godson." Sergeant Bilko ends up in a college classroom himself with a young student, and I was hired as an extra to be a student, and I checked with the director, "Where's Mr. Silvers gonna sit?" The director told me and so I grabbed the chair next to him. I tapped my pencil and I heard that later Silvers said, "Who's the kid who knew to tap the pencil and steal the scene?" Milton Berle said, "Always have something to be doing to bring the eyes to you" and it's true, be straightening your tie, straightening the flap on your pocket, checking for dust on the table.

"Exactly true," said I as someone who has spent many a day backgrounding, as they call it. Actually, only a few days before my conversation with Dick, my remote control stumbled upon me waiting for an elevator with Katie Holmes and Paul Dano in *The Extra Man*, and a few days prior to that, someone pointed out they saw me approaching a revolving door at Sotheby's with Nicole Kidman in *Rabbit Hole.*

Dick is synonymous with his show, and *The Dick Cavett Show* has been woven into several films over the years. Perhaps, best known is the brilliantly edited clip of Cavett chatting with both John Lennon and Forrest Gump.

I know. I get all the worst parts of movies, said Dick in his best deadpan.

I then mentioned the extended clip of an actual Cavett monologue from the spring of 1970. It is featured in *Apollo 13* when Ken Mattingly, the astronaut portrayed by Gary Sinise, who had to stay home because they thought he had measles, is sitting in his apartment, obviously frustrated, and he's watching Cavett tell jokes about the mission to the moon. I also brought up a fabulous piece of movie-making from the film *Frequency*. The sci-fi film revolves around a father and son talking to each other via ham radio. The father exists in 1969, the now adult son in 1999, and in one scene, as they are talking to one another, each has their television on in their respective living rooms; both are tuned to a contemporary Cavett show. Dick has the same guest on the show in '69 as he does in '99, and you see the two different episodes in the background of the scene. In terms of filmmaking, it's just a really cool technique to set the two periods apart yet create an artistic symmetry.

Whenever I look at my list of movies, you'd think I was a movie actor. There's one called Moon Over Parador, *which was directed by Paul Mazursky, and there's another one in which I'm Cavett again, directed by John Frankenheimer, called* The Day of the Gun. *Yet* Beetlejuice, *it seems to be, is the one where I have the most to do, I guess.*

At this point, I searched my mind if there was anything else I wanted to chat about with Dick. What immediately presented itself just seemed to drop from my brain and fire out over the tongue. It was a line that must've sounded scripted, but it wasn't. It was an improvisation of the heart.

"I have to tell you, Dick, right now, I feel like a graffiti artist getting the chance to sit at the foot of Michelangelo; this has been quite a treat for me, it truly has."

Can I use that line?

"Yes, but just say, 'Kalegi told me I could use it,' and we'll be fine," I replied with a bit of a snicker.

Dick then interrupted my on-air goodbye with what could only be called a true Cavettism: *Do you have to go through your life saying "Kalegi, spelled the usual way?"*

I decided to play along as it was time to swim in the deep end of the conversational pool: "Yeah, quite often. It's been mispronounced, but it's very easy: kuh-LEG-ee. People have said, why don't you change your name? Well, I don't want to. I'm me and proud to be me."

Yeah, nothing's wrong with Ed. said Dick through a true verbal wink. *What, are you gonna be? Hawthorne Kalegi?*

There it was: the pitch-perfect way to end my conversation with Dick Cavett.

"Dick, thank you so much for joining me."

Thank you, Ed. We must celebrate this someday over a glass of beer.

The studio engineer ended the recording, and I took a moment off-air to thank Dick for being so gracious with his time and engaging in his conversation. That authoritative yet melodious voice laced with just enough midwestern charm to match his urbane and sensitive sophistication seemed to genuinely enjoy our time together. Dick then went off to continue his day. Right then, I took notice of my body language. I unknowingly lounged back into the studio seat and pulled the mic closer to meet my slouch as I nursed a large, cold Dunkin Donuts coffee. My ankles were crossed one over the other as my feet dangled over a crate placed under the console. Wow, I had channeled the relaxed spirit of Katherine Hepburn! You see what talking to Cavett does to someone?

I gathered my stuff, left the radio station, and began the long ride home. This is when I normally replay what I've just recorded in my mind. I'm always hyper-critical when I analyze from short-term memory what I've just done. But I do have to say, I was quite satisfied with the Cavett conversation. More than anything, it struck me as I sat at a red light that I had just spoken with that man I watched on that tiny snowy Sony black and white screen all those years ago, and at that point, for some peculiar and unknown, yet very strong reason, I wished I still had that old TV with the broken antenna and terrible vertical hold.

Oh, and by the way, it is Kalegi, spelled the usual way.

19

Lizz Winstead

Comedian, Activist, Co-Creator of *The Daily Show*

People are like, "Oh, well, you're just singing to the choir." And I always say, "You know, the choir can always use more songs."

***

Comedy has changed dramatically over the past quarter century, especially in late night. Beginning in 1954, when NBC took a local show in New York hosted by Steve Allen, put it on the network, and called it *Tonight*, late-night television spent the next half century night after night essentially churning out the same type of shows. The formula included about ten to fifteen minutes of non-offensive humor, very brief and extremely innocuous references to events in the real world, followed by a few guests doing their familiar acts and routines in bursts of very light conversation. Steve Allen invented it, Johnny Carson perfected it, and David Letterman modernized it. Two men, Jack Paar and Dick Cavett, tried to inject issues and substantive political humor into the format and were somewhat successful at it but, in each case, only for brief periods of time. The comedy and content of Allen, Carson, and Letterman, while wildly successful, was also frustratingly disposable.

Be it Steve Allen doing his show atop a pole overlooking a street corner, Carson predictably plodding through another Carnac bit, or Letterman reading yet another Top Ten List, it may have made you chuckle, but it rarely made you think. Jay Leno's version of *The Tonight Show* beginning in 1992 brought little if anything to help evolve the format and by the late '90s, Letterman was doing very much the same show on CBS that he was doing on NBC back in the late '80s. Late night had hit a rut, a chasm of comedy with little true purpose. But change was on the horizon, thanks to two women. I had the opportunity to chat with one of them.

It was great to say hello to Lizz Winstead.

It was on July 22, 1996, when *The Daily Show* premiered on Comedy Central, co-created by Lizz Winstead and Madeleine Smithberg. At first, the show was a bit tempered in its political focus, mainly because of its initial host. Craig Kilborn was a hip, young ESPN *Sportscenter* anchor who, like many of the ESPN personalities of the time, was too cool for school, had cringeworthy catchphrases, and who all seemed to be trying to get out of sports and into comedy. Kilborn, to his credit, got his chance to escape sports via *The Daily Show* and three years later turned that into a network opportunity when he replaced Tom Snyder in the 12:30 slot on CBS following Letterman.

Kilborn was all about pop culture and entertainment as he attempted to be a cooler and even more esoteric West Coast incarnation of Conan O'Brien. He had little interest in politics, opinions, and the events of the day. Kilborn's departure from *The Daily Show* opened the door for comedian Jon Stewart to take over the role as host. All of a sudden, the day's headlines became the creative foundation of a late-night talk show that featured a host with a true point of view who used comedy to entertain a much more politically engaged and socially aware audience. Television and its sensitivities had moved far away from Don Rickles telling racist jokes to a studio audience of 200 fifty-year-olds while Johnny Carson giggled through a blue cloud of cigarette smoke. I began my conversation with Lizz wanting to learn about her belief in comedy with a purpose.

"Lizz, I've always thought of you as someone who led the contemporary movement to the concept and approach of comedy having a purpose. I think back to when I was a kid, I'd sit and I'd watch *The Tonight Show,* and I'd see what seemed to me as disposable comedy, and I'm not saying that in a bad way, but it was just comedy thrown out there. It was like, here's David Brenner. Now, here's the setup, the punchline, the laugh, another setup, another punchline, another laugh. It didn't have any lasting meaning. When did you realize that, for you, comedy needed to be purposeful?"

Well, Ed, I think we used to live in a time where comedy was escapism, and you could literally live in the world and you could laugh at things that were mundane. At some point, all of that changed for me and I started doing a sort of political comedy. My act started out as observational, but then during the first Gulf War, when it just seemed like cable news was just wall to wall one-sided coverage, it didn't really seem like we were getting all the information.

Lizz went on to tell me that, in her act, she began to stress that perhaps we should begin to find out more on our own and become curious about the world around us, the events that drive it, and the information we consume about it. It was the gateway to being able to joke about hypocrisy, which is a pretty obvious seedling for the type of comedy that would become the foundation of *The Daily Show.* She also mentioned how that brand of comedy spurs political interest and participation. Since the mid-2000s, our entertainment and our comedy, especially late-night television, has become rooted in the politics of the day. I don't believe it's any great coincidence that the younger generation is now engaged to the point where they speak out, they participate, and they vote. They matter and now use their collective voice very effectively. College-aged people up through those in their early thirties have become much more activist in nature, in great part due to political opinion becoming a major tenet of contemporary comedy.

I think the true key in all of it when you use humor is that you have to be a reliable narrator. And what I mean by that is you need to have your facts right. But in addition, you can't be one-sided. If somebody you like messes up, whether they use their power for their idiocy or they use their power corruptly, you have to call everybody out. Otherwise, you're just gonna be partisan.

It's important for me here to stress that shows such as *The Daily Show*, especially once Jon Stewart took over as host, as well as Stephen Colbert, John Oliver, Jimmy Kimmel, and even *Saturday Night Live* do tend to be one-sided in their opinions and in who they choose to skewer. These shows are not friendly to conservative audiences. Then again, that points to the key demographics of these shows which tend to be younger and better educated. They are simply super serving their audience which simply makes good business sense. Conservatives found their own late-night personality in Greg Gutfeld on the Fox News Channel, but Gutfeld's presentation strikes me as different. While the others I just cited tend to present their views through a traditional prism of comedy, Gutfeld seems to communicate through a "get off my lawn" veneer that comes off as not only snarky but a bit nasty as well. To each his own, I guess.

Lizz believes that lampooning true hypocrisy knows no political boundaries. If you can target a hypocrisy which strikes a common chord, you can reach any audience with any political proclivity.

I think it's fun to be gathered in a room if you feel upset about what's happening in the world, began Lizz, *and be able to come to a show where some of that is going to be addressed. This is especially true when we're in cities sometimes like Birmingham or Little Rock where, if your political leanings are center left, you may not find your people as readily. So, to be able to come to a room with 300 to 400 people who are laughing at hypocrisy with you, that's kind of great.*

I couldn't resist once I heard Lizz mention, in the hypothetical, *if your political leanings are center-left.* Lizz Winstead's personal politics lie quite left of center, thus if she were performing in Birmingham or Little Rock, her brand of political humor might raise a red state eyebrow or two.

"You brought up performing in places like Birmingham and Little Rock, and I'm thinking you run the risk of getting a couple of nasty looks the next morning at the breakfast bar at the Holiday Inn. Do you not?"

Of course, and you know, that's the whole thing. It's why I like to be sort of loud and proud about my belief system, so nobody feels hoodwinked. I can avoid it when people are like, "Oh, well, you're just singing to the choir." And I always say, you know, the choir can always use more songs. I'm a comedian whose politics are out there. I'm left of center, and I like to be really upfront about it so that, when I perform, folks can be like, "Oh, that's what that is, I'm gonna go see that," or "I don't want any part of that. No, thank you." So, yeah, I think that if I open up my computer laptop at the breakfast bar at the Hampton Inn down south and they see all my stickers on the outside of it, I get some side-eye for sure.

Lizz went on to say that she's fine with that side-eye reaction. She feels that sometimes it can open a dialogue and emphasizes that it's always good to speak one's truth because, if not, it becomes difficult to effect change. But as Lizz told me that, I realized she, somewhat sneakily, upgraded her accommodations in our theoretical lodging references.

"You just did something very surreptitious," I said. "You upgraded your hotel. I had you in a Holiday Inn, and all of a sudden, you're down the road at the Hampton Inn, which is a nicer place. That's a hell of a nice move there, Winstead. I like that very much. That was good."

Lizz cracked up, laughing quite loudly, and then explained why she had Hampton and not Holiday on her mind.

Can I tell you the story? This is why I mentioned Hampton Inn: not to give a plug to anybody, but I once stayed in a Hampton Inn, and the manager of the Hampton Inn Googled me. When I got to my room, they had a framed picture of my dogs in my room and a note which read, "I'm guessing you're gonna miss your furry friends, so we printed out pictures of them for your room," and I thought that that was really cool.

"Wow, that's either really cool or really creepy when you think about it."

I know. I told one person who thought it was cool and another who did think it was wicked creepy. But if I'm on Google, which I am, and it comes up that I am pro-choice and I'm an activist, I could get really creepy pictures framed and put into my room. But instead, I got cute pictures of my dog. So, I felt good about that.

So now whenever I'm on TripAdvisor scrolling through reviews of some random Hampton Inn somewhere, and I see a rave entry exclaiming how great it is that they print out pictures of your pets and have them waiting, framed in your room, I'll know that's Lizz Winstead.

"I'll tell you what, Lizz, the Hampton Inn, and again, not to endorse a hotel, but their breakfast is very good."

Yes, they have a good breakfast.

"Oh my God, don't they," I asked only somewhat rhetorically as I became a bit too excited about a free breakfast. "You go down in the morning, and they're gettin' the food out there. The eggs disappear? Boom. There are new eggs in two seconds. I'm never standing there looking for some pancake goo to make a waffle or whatever. It's great. I love it, and now that I know you get framed pictures of dogs, that's even better."

Lizz then stunted my culinary excitement and unpaid endorsement of Hampton Inn with her own breakfast story from an off-brand hotel.

I like to waffle, and you have to be careful because one time, I went to this off-brand hotel, and instead of having actual waffle batter, they had something called Batter Blast.

"Eww," I said with my mind involuntarily directed to places I'd prefer not to talk about.

It is an aerosol batter and you spray this batter into the waffle iron.

"Good God," I said with a noticeably increasing horrified disgust in my tone.

I'm telling you, Ed, I was traumatized.

"Lizz, now I know what happened to brands such as Adorn and Aqua Net from back in the '80s that started out making hairspray. Nowadays, they're making pancake batter that's sprayed out via an aerosol can."

That's right, and it's non-stick and comes in chocolate too!

At this point, I pivoted away from a place in the conversation I never thought we'd be, instead talking about Lizz's upbringing.

"We all know what your politics are. You grew up in Minneapolis, but I read you're the youngest child born into a very conservative Catholic family. So, it begs the question, what the hell happened?"

You know, it's like if you live in Minneapolis and you're conservative, that is in and of itself a bizarro world because Minneapolis is a very liberal city. My dad grew up outside of Meridian, Mississippi, and he met my mom during World War II. He often called Minnesota the People's Republic of Minnesota, so he was always super conservative. I'm the youngest kid, so I have Vietnam War-era siblings. There was always toxic politics and fighting at the table. And then my mom, a good Catholic woman, insisted we go to a Catholic grade school, which then became run by Jesuits, and they were quite liberal. She was trying to give us a good Catholic conservative upbringing, but she just kept introducing liberalism by accident into it. And I'll never forget my dad saying to me, "Dammit, I raised you to have an opinion, and I forgot to tell you it was supposed to be mine."

That opinion led to a viewpoint that led to the creation of a television show that changed the way a generation looks at entertainment, their country, and their leaders and spurred a critical interest in the world in which they lived. Lizz Winstead is one of the key architects of activist comedy. It is comedy with purpose, meaning, and intent. Late-night television has never been the same and we are now eons removed from the non-political nights of Johnny Carson all those years ago. Comedy clubs are now ripe with societal and political sarcasm and that is eons removed from Jerry Seinfeld wondering why peanuts given out on airplanes are so small.

I thanked Lizz for her time and for a great conversation.

That was so much fun, Ed, you are so smart!

Maybe there's hope for me after all.

20

Ken Levine

Emmy and Writers' Guild Award-Winning Writer and Major League Baseball Announcer

Characters always drive the story as far as I'm concerned.

***

When we're kids, and our parents ask us what we want to be when we grow up, we always tend to respond with great bravado and list some rather unrealistic and pie-in-the-sky career endeavors: space traveler, NFL football player, President of the United States, famous Hollywood actor, rock star, etc. I don't know how Ken Levine answered that question back in the 1950s, but if he said something about writing some of the most memorable episodic television in history and doing play-by-play for a few Major League Baseball teams, he would've proved himself to be quite clairvoyant.

If Ken's name looks familiar, it's because you've seen it flash on the screen at the beginning of dozens of episodes of some of America's favorite television shows, including *M*A*S*H, Cheers,* and *Frasier.* Many of the most memorable and instantly recognizable lines quipped by Hawkeye Pierce, Sam Malone, and Frasier Crane are the product of Ken's genius. His wit and words have shaped our entertainment for years and his ability behind a microphone has added texture to many broadcasts of Baltimore Orioles, Seattle Mariners, and San Diego Padres baseball games.

His resume is something most other people can only dream of. Ken is the epitome of professional accomplishment: two dream careers that each took great advantage of his ability to craft and tell wonderful stories with words, his words.

It was great to say hello to Ken Levine.

As I settled in behind the studio microphone awaiting Ken's call, I began to wonder where to best begin our conversation. So many shows, so many episodes, then the parallel career as a baseball announcer. That's quite a palette, crowded with as many colors as Bob Ross always seemed to have at the ready. All of that creativity had to start somewhere, and it had to come from someplace. Then it hit me.

"Ken, what ignited your creative fire? What made you want to write in the first place?"

I guess it was the narcissistic need to express myself. When I was a kid growing up watching The Dick Van Dyke Show, *I was in love with Laura Petrie, and the lightbulb went off over my head. It's like, wait a minute, you don't have to be a football player to get a girl like Laura Petrie? You can be a comedy writer?!? Hey, maybe there's hope for me yet.*

There you have it: America, one of the more prolific writers in television history, was captivated by Mary Tyler Moore's capri pants. Then again, so were many others at the time.

Oh, baby, it made me wanna run to the typewriter! Ken exclaimed with a chuckle.

Ken's journey to becoming a writer, albeit jump-started by the image of Laura Petrie, didn't begin with the written word but with the spoken. During the 1960s, there was something captivating about Top 40 AM Radio. It radiated with excitement, and there was fun. It seemed as if the person whose voice was heard between the latest Beatles and Beach Boys hits had the greatest job in the world. If you lived in New York, it was WABC, in Chicago, it was WLS, and the big station where Ken grew up was KHJ in Los Angeles. Ken was captivated as well; he had contracted the radio bug. But I wanted to know, even after acknowledging his narcissistic need to express himself through writing, why did he decide that radio was the best place to start?

Well, Ed, I loved radio, and I loved originally just hearing Vin Scully calling Dodger games and then hearing other radio personalities in Southern California. Usually, the ones I was attracted to were the ones who were funny, like Gary Owens, or Loman and Barkley, Robert W. Morgan, Emperor Hudson. It just seemed like a really fun career, so I got involved with the campus radio station.

But when Ken left college and embarked on a career as a Top 40 DJ, he found himself on a career path laced with more stopovers than a cross-country Greyhound bus route. He, as many others, bounced around the country from market to market. It didn't take long for Ken to reassess the likelihood of finding stability and great fortune in music radio.

It's a fun gig to have if, number one, you don't mind being fired and moving every four months and, number two, you're in your early twenties. This is not the kind of career that you go: man, do I wanna be 60 years old, still playing "Pretty Woman" by Roy Orbison? So, I kind of reached a point when I was like 23 or 24, where I thought to myself, this is not the best career choice.

I then pointed out to Ken that even as a disc jockey, thoughts of sitcoms were obviously never far from his mind. Many radio DJs, especially during the heyday of Top 40, used hip-sounding fake names while on the air. Sorry to burst your bubble, but the Jack family didn't really name their son Wolfman. Ken's on-air name was Beaver Cleaver, a clever way to pay homage to *Leave It to Beaver*, but was that Ken's reason for using it?

When I went to WDRQ in Detroit, I thought, you know what? I want a name that stands out. I want a name that's easy to say, and I want a name that the minute the audience hears it, they perk up and go, Beaver Cleaver? Of course, I wanted them to wonder whether I was the guy on the TV show, but it just gave me a chance to distinguish myself. Plus, I was able to do a lot of cheap double entendres using the name.

"Uh, yeah, that's true," I said, realizing at that moment the double entendre opportunity to which Ken was referring. I then pivoted in order to maintain the PG-13 rating of the show. The one thing that continues to fascinate me most about Ken Levine's writing career is how fast he established himself in Hollywood. In 1975, Ken and his writing partner David Issacs sold a script for *The Jeffersons*, which was a spinoff of *All in the Family* and a very popular show in its own right. I asked Ken how he and David were able to not just start but start quite big.

Well, in those days, there were really only three networks. So, it's kind of like saying there's the major leagues but no minor leagues. Now you have cable shows and streaming shows and there are way more venues that you can crack. But back then you pretty much had to either break in with the Yankees or you didn't play Major League Baseball, and we were very lucky as I had quit radio. I came back to Los Angeles and was working at a broadcast school teaching kids how to tell time on the radio.

David and I would get together on weekends and three or four nights a week, and we would write our spec scripts, and we figured, okay, we're gonna give it two years and figure that somebody along the way is gonna recognize that we have a modicum of talent. We were very lucky that we were able to get our script to the story editor of The Jeffersons, *Gordon Mitchell. He invited us to come in and pitch stories for the show, and they liked one and bought it. That was the start, and once you sell a script and you're in the Writer's Guild, you can get a decent agent. Things really started taking off from there. We still kept our day jobs, though, for about six months after we sold our first script.*

Yeah, but Ken Levine didn't need that day job teaching kids how to tell time on the radio for much longer. Ken began a long run on *M*A*S*H*, where he became the head writer at 28. Ken understood that show quite well: the cadence, the tone, the underlying message. I asked Ken why *M*A*S*H* was such a good fit. He said it was because he had been in the Army Reserves. Ken explained that the draft was still in place, and in order to avoid being sent to Vietnam, he managed to get himself into an Armed Forces Radio Reserve unit.

Looking back at it, it turned out to be the best thing that ever happened to me because I met my partner David, in the Army Reserve Unit, and without the background of being in the military, I don't think I could have written M*A*S*H *with any authority and* M*A*S*H *is really what launched my career. So, if you're a young person and you want to write comedy, join the Marines, I guess.*

"Wow, that's a heck of a commercial for the military," I remarked. "Head down to the recruiting center this afternoon, and in only three and a half years, you'll be writing screenplays and be a huge star in Hollywood!"

But what am I doing in Iraq? Ken said with a sarcastic snicker in his voice.

Oh well, so much for my impromptu ad campaign to increase enlistments. Anyway, *M*A*S*H* is how I first became aware of Ken, seeing his name in the credits as they flashed on the screen during the opening scenes of so many of the episodes. Ken worked on *M*A*S*H* seasons five through eight and the show, in my opinion, seemed to grow up a bit and truly hit a deeper tone during that time. New characters such as BJ and Charles and Colonel Potter had just been introduced, and the show seemed to go in deeper and more meaningful directions. Even the character of Margaret was broadened and completely fleshed out. She was no longer "Hot Lips" Houlihan, she was Major Margaret Houlihan and the scripts and storylines created a character with more substance and one given much more respect. I mentioned these thoughts to Ken, and he agreed with my take.

Ed, I think you're right. Everyone wanted to explore these characters a little bit more and really get to know them better. And it was really a balancing act because we wanted to, as you say, deepen the show, but we didn't want to lose that sense of anarchy and that whimsy and that level of comedy that had been established early on by Larry Gelbart and Gene Reynolds. So, for us, it was a balancing act to try to keep both things going at once.

*M*A*S*H* was also rather unique in how it was produced. In the mid to late 1970s, there weren't many thirty-minute shows that used the one-camera approach and were shot without the presence of a live studio audience. While Norman Lear's and Garry Marshall's shows were shot with a three-camera set-up on a soundstage in front of a live and sometimes boisterous studio audience, *M*A*S*H,* the television series, stayed quite true to the film upon which it was based. It used the one-camera approach used in filmmaking; many scenes were shot outdoors on a set that dovetailed perfectly with the permanent indoor sets, and even after a while, the canned laugh track was discarded. *M*A*S*H* was also a show that was unafraid and would look to break new ground, even if just for a single episode.

A season seven episode titled "Point of View" takes the audience through an episode-long first-person journey showing what it was like to be a patient at the 4077th. It was extremely unique to anything else being done on television, seeing the actors speak directly to the camera and to us, their collective patient. Another example, which ironically, I just happened to stumble upon while clicking around my remote control the morning I chatted with Ken, is an episode titled "Our Finest Hour," where journalist Clete Roberts visits the 4077th to shoot a documentary about Army life during the Korean War. The interview portions were filmed in black and white to mimic what it would've looked like in the early '50s. These two episodes, which I referenced to Ken, came along pretty deep into the series' run, so it made me wonder: how challenging is it to be innovative within a series when that series is already so well tethered and entrenched?

The problem for us was that the series was so well-established that you really couldn't move the characters. You couldn't let them grow in the way that you could with most series where characters get married, and then they move to a different apartment, and then they have kids, and the series really evolves. These characters were locked in time and space in Korea, and at the 4077th, we were looking for different ways to tell their story. "Point of View" was an episode that my partner and I wrote. We said to Burt Metcalf, who was the showrunner when we pitched it, this is either gonna be the best or worst episode of the year. It's either gonna work, or it's not. It was something we saw when doing a little research in a movie from, I believe, from the forties called Lady in the Lake *with Robert Montgomery. It was shot point-of-view, so this technique isn't something we invented. And when we wrote the episode, what we found was that when characters talked to the patient, who was essentially the viewer of the episode, it was fine. But when the patient talks to the other characters, they're just standing on the screen listening. It was weird and very awkward. So that gave us the idea, why don't we make the injury something to the throat so the patient can't talk and thus we eliminate that problem? That proved to be very, very helpful.*

I will say two more things about "Point of View." Number one, you can't talk about that show without heaping enough praise on Charlie Dubin, who directed it, especially because back then, those were the days before minicams and lightweight cameras. They were huge, bulky 35-millimeter cameras that he had to schlep around and position in just the right way. Number two, when we saw the final product on a big screen because we would screen the episode in a screening room, there were these giant heads, and we thought, oh my God, this is horrid. This is unbelievably terrible. What did we do? But when we watched it on TV and all of a sudden Radar's head was on a 19-inch TV and not on a 200-foot screen, it suddenly all worked like a charm. But, going into it, I thought, this is gonna be the biggest embarrassment of our career. Thankfully it was not."

I then remembered another *M*A*S*H* episode written by Ken, the two-part episode *"Goodbye Radar,"* which was important on many different levels because it ends the story of a seminal character, which is quite a responsibility of reverence.

"Ken," I asked, "were there any special challenges in dealing with that, in writing Radar off the show?"

Well, the one thing that we tried to do, and it's interesting, is that we consciously avoided a lot of what they did years later in the final episode. We did not want there to be a lot of maudlin speeches. And so, we purposely designed it so that there were casualties arriving in the camp, and ultimately, Radar had to say goodbye to everybody on the run. So, the moments were very brief and my favorite moment in the show, there's no dialogue at all. It's the tag at the end when Hawkeye, and I know spoiler alert, when Hawkeye and BJ come back to the Swamp after 24 hours of O.R., and there's Radar's teddy bear sitting on Hawkeye's bunk. It symbolizes how he grew up.

It's funny how the mind works, or at least the way my mind works. As Ken was describing his process in writing "Goodbye Radar," I began playing the tape of that episode via the VHS player in my brain. I recalled the scene where Hawkeye and Radar see each other for the final time. Radar peers through that dirty little window in the door looking into the operating room while Hawkeye is working on a patient. Radar and Hawkeye salute each other. Radar appears stoic and turns away from the door. I always felt it was handled so well, and it was the perfect way to send Radar, now a man, back to Ottumwa, Iowa, to provide for his family.

"Ken, I think that was a wonderful way to end that relationship and complete Radar's story."

Thanks. We had established that Hawkeye had an irreverence and would not salute officers. You know, that was his big thing. He wouldn't salute generals; he wouldn't salute officers. So, for him to salute Radar was a big gesture on his part. And again, it's simple, it's just behavior, no long speeches. People weren't crying, people weren't hugging. It just seemed to be more elegant to us.

Elegant indeed. At this point in our conversation, I decided to change the geography from Korea to Boston and take a trip with Ken to *Cheers*. As a sitcom, *Cheers* always seemed a bit unique to me because it was many things. It was a workplace comedy, it was a romantic comedy, and it was a show about a group of people who became a pseudo family for one another. It was also an indelible part of 1980s and early 1990s pop culture, a show which truly looks, breathes, and sounds like the times from which it came. I asked Ken to define why *Cheers* worked as well as it did.

I think the planets aligned, and we were able to hire the perfect cast. I think if you don't have Ted Danson and you don't have Shelley Long in that first year, I don't know if the show lasts more than 13 episodes. The writing was terrific. Glen and Les Charles are brilliant writers, and there's something very inviting about that bar and that whole atmosphere. It really was a place that you wanted to be in. I always thought Taxi *was a great show but never really got the long-standing love that I thought it deserved. And I always maintained the problem was that it was set in this grimy garage, and you just didn't want to go to that garage every week.*

But you did want to go to Cheers. *You did want to be one of those people hanging out at the bar, being at* Cheers. *So there was a certain amount of verisimilitude, some, you know, wish fulfillment. I think a lot of that was true with* Cheers. *But I, I don't know, there was something kind of magical about that show. My partner and I were on it for nine years. We wrote 40 episodes of* Cheers, *and we never got tired of writing those characters."*

"Ken," I jumped in, "perhaps it's because those characters also deepened to such an extent that you were allowed to explore different things and go different places with each of those characters."

Well, that's true, and in the same way that we would deepen characters in M*A*S*H, *you wanted to know more about them. When a show begins, you want the characters to just be identifiable. So, it's like, oh, okay, I see who she is. I see who he is, I see what their relationship is. Okay, got it. But once you get past that, then you want to get underneath the jokes and see who really is Carla Tortelli and who really is Frasier Crane. That's part of the fun of the show to me: exploring those things and taking these characters on a journey and kind of unpeeling the onion and finding out more about them. Wow, if I used enough cliches in one sentence there.*

Wow, what do I do here? Do I agree and thereby backhandedly admonish one of the most prolific screenwriters in television history that, yes, he did stray at least somewhat into cliche purgatory? Hell no, your humble host is a bit too diplomatic for such an egregious transgression.

"No, it's all good, Ken," I said with a reassuring chuckle in my voice, "they all dovetailed and it worked perfectly." I figured it was a good time to ask Ken the question I've asked many writers and authors over the years: "Ken, does the story drive the characters, or do the characters drive the story?

Characters always drive the story as far as I'm concerned. We never think in terms of plot. We think in terms of the characters. What do they want? What do they need? Why can't they get it? Those are the questions that we ask, we never think in terms of, okay, we need a story about this, a story about that. That's why it's always hard when we have things like Christmas stories where you go, alright we gotta do a Christmas story somehow. It's not nearly as organic as, oh, what about if Sam has this issue? What about if Sam and Diane have differing views about this issue and build a show around that?

Out of all the episodes of all the shows that Ken Levine's pen has scripted, if he had to choose one as his favorite, which would it be?

Ken immediately replied without hesitation. "Point of View" *from M*A*S*H. It's hard to top.*

I then decided to explore with Ken how what we watch is presented and consumed in such dramatically different ways in the 2020s than it was in the '70s, '80s, and '90s. We have so many choices today, it's almost ridiculous. My new Hamilton Beach microwave oven came with its own streaming app. For only $6.95 a month I can simultaneously watch both *Mannix* and *90 Day Fiancé* if I look a certain way into the microwave's window. There is so much content, both professional and amateur, on so many platforms. There is no longer appointment television or "Must See Thursdays on NBC," we now scatter into corners, cubicles, Ubers, all within our own segmented worlds to watch whatever, whenever. I was interested in Ken's take on this and when I asked the question, I pretty much knew the gist of what his answer would be, but I wanted to give him his chance to take the metaphorical megaphone and stand on the soapbox I had just built.

"What have we lost when it comes to folks watching at different times and on all kinds of devices? Is that a bad thing or is that a good thing?"

No, Ed, I think that's a bad thing because I really miss our shared events and it seems like now pretty much the Super Bowl is our only annual shared event. It used to be the Oscars, but, you know, not anymore. The numbers for the Oscars are way down. Numbers for other award shows are even worse. The World Series used to be a big deal, now it's not. The Olympics used to be a big deal and, yeah it gets okay ratings, but not the way it used to where the entire country was enthralled for two weeks. I think as a society, as a community, we need events and things to bring us together. Instead, everything now is so fractionalized. I think it's very unfortunate.

At this point, I pivoted to what became a parallel career for Ken, that as a Major League Baseball announcer. I remembered that earlier in our conversation, Ken mentioned how he was influenced at an early age by listening to Vin Scully broadcast Dodgers games after the team relocated from Brooklyn to Los Angeles. In addition to Scully, 30 miles down the road in Anaheim, Ken had the benefit of listening to Dick Enberg broadcast Angels games. Outside of Howard Cosell, Enberg was probably the most popular and versatile network sportscaster in America in the 1970s and 1980s as the lead announcer for NBC Sports.

"Ken, it's the mid-1980s, and you're in the middle of a great career as a screenwriter. What made you want to change course and become a Major League Baseball announcer?"

Well, I guess you could call it a midlife crisis, and I had reached a point where we had just finished creating a year-long series for Mary Tyler Moore, and that was a, let's just say, a rugged experience. I figured if I don't pursue this now, I never will and so I went with a tape recorder to the upper deck of Dodger Stadium and for two years just recorded games into a tape recorder and learned how to do baseball play-by-play and sent tapes around the minor leagues. I was hired and spent three years in the minors, one year in Syracuse and two years in Tidewater, Virginia, all the while I'm still on Cheers. *Even when I was announcing baseball games, I was writing scripts and sending them in. Then there was an opening in 1991 for the Baltimore Orioles, I sent in my tape and got the job.*

Ken told me what he relished more than actually doing the play-by-play of the games was experiencing the lifestyle of a baseball announcer: to be with a team, to travel with a team, to experience what it's like to get up in the morning and the only responsibility you have is to go to a ballpark that night and call a baseball game.

Even if I didn't get to the big leagues, I still would have walked away from the experience without calling it a failure. Getting to the big leagues was an amazing gift.

Now, let me explain the process for those who may not understand. It's not really that easy to get hired as a professional baseball announcer. Even back when Ken struck gold rather quickly in his quest, it was quite the herculean task to be given the chance to call baseball games for a living. The competition has always been tremendous. Every young sportscaster fresh out of their college radio station, sportswriters who yearned to be behind a microphone and not a typewriter, the sports guy on the six o'clock news, as well as the folks who persistently hung around the periphery of the industry were constantly bombarding every minor and major league team with their audition tapes. The fact that Ken got in and got in with relative ease is quite astonishing.

"You got to the big leagues relatively quickly," I began, "and you landed in the Orioles radio booth, where you were working with some incredibly talented announcers: Jon Miller and Chuck Thompson. Chuck Thompson had one of the best radio baseball voices I've ever heard. He was silk on crushed velvet with a little velour mixed in. There are old air checks on YouTube and what I love, when you listen to some of those early '70s Orioles games, is you could tell that Chuck was quite a stickler for both elocution and pronunciation. He always made a point to pronounce the two T's, the N before the M and the U before the N D in Merv Rettenmund. His voice was synonymous with Orioles baseball at that time. I also remember seeing somewhere a long time ago, and correct me if I'm wrong about this, you replaced Joe Angel with the Orioles, didn't you also replace him years earlier at one of your radio jobs?"

I did, indeed. I replaced Joe at KMEN in San Bernardino as a disc jockey, and then I replaced him in the Orioles booth. And you're right about Chuck Thompson, what a gentleman, you know, so elegant, I learned so much from him. My other partner, Jon Miller, what a gorgeous instrument he has for a voice. Imagine you're with Jon Miller and Chuck Thompson and you don't have the best voice in the broadcast booth, I'm like Mickey Mouse.

I then told Ken that I believed what made him the perfect human extension of a baseball microphone was that inherent to the job of baseball play-by-play is the ability to tell a story and tell it well. It requires the ability to weave stories into the fabric of the game itself. As a screenwriter, Ken is a born storyteller. He simply took his talent of telling a story within a 22-minute television episode and used it to fully flesh out a nine-inning ballgame. Neither is easy, but Ken was excellent at both.

"So, for you, Ken, to take those two elements: the ability to tell a story and tell it succinctly and with good language and good choices, and to do that within a baseball game, you had to think to yourself while in the moment, that this was simply a perfect situation, was it not?"

Oh, absolutely. People ask, well, what's the difference between writing and calling a baseball game? Well, they're both storytelling. The only difference is, I can't change the ending of a baseball game. I can't go back and rewrite it. But, storytelling, that's what I love about baseball as opposed to other sports because I've also called basketball and once you get the glossary down and once you understand the game, then the ebb and flow of the action just carries you along back and forth down the court. But when you're announcing baseball, you have lots of time to kill and I don't have Chuck Thompson's voice, but I had a personality and a storytelling ability and a sense of humor. Hopefully my broadcasts were entertaining as well as informative and accurate.

I spoke with Ken just before the start of the Major League Baseball season and this was the season where a pitch clock was being implemented and for the first time ever, the pitcher needed to deliver the ball in a certain amount of time. It was quite a controversial idea for baseball traditionalists, so I asked Ken for his opinion.

I love it. I absolutely love it. Because it was starting to take so long. When the Dodgers first came to Los Angeles, their owner Walter O'Malley was worried that people couldn't get to the ballpark until late because of all of the freeway traffic. Dodger games in LA started at eight o'clock at night and were over at 10:30. Until the introduction of the time clock, they'd start at seven o'clock at night and end at 11. This is crazy, and I think anything that baseball can do to move things along is a good thing. Pitchers don't need all that time between pitches. I was talking to Eric Nadel, who is the Hall of Fame voice of the Texas Rangers. He told me a couple of years ago, there was like a stretch in a game of 22 minutes in an inning between batted balls being put into play between foul balls, conferences, new pitchers, walks, and throws over to first base. That's insane.

I agree with Ken, the pitch clock has infused an energy into the game which had been lost and in a world of shorter attention spans, thousands of diversions, and more choices for entertainment than ever before, Major League Baseball needed to do something to bring the sport into the reality which is the 2020s.

At this point, the clock on the wall stared me down and told me it was time to say goodbye to Ken Levine. I told Ken that he was truly a bucket list guest for me, and it was fun getting to know someone who has created lines and dialogue, which still lives within all of us all these years later.

"Ken, I've enjoyed this so much. Thank you for joining me."

My pleasure, Ed.

I then left the studio, ate dinner, and settled in that evening for a few episodes of *M*A*S*H* to celebrate a truly great conversation.

I love my job.

21

Rob Burnett

Writer and Director. Executive Producer of *The Late Show with David Letterman* and former President of Worldwide Pants

I wouldn't trade it for the world, and I don't think I would do it again for the world, either.

***

When you watch television, it all looks so easy, doesn't it? It all looks so seamless. Everything always appears to go off without a hitch. Well, that's usually because of the people who toil behind the camera, not in front of it. True, there needs to be top-shelf talent that attracts an audience and keeps it, but the finer elements of any show are usually the work of those behind the scenes who are never seen by the viewers. Late-night TV is its own special animal: five shows a week, usually taped only a few hours prior to air, with different guests and new comedy elements every night.

Being the Executive Producer of a late-night show is quite a job, with tremendous responsibility, and I had a chance to talk about it with the long-time EP of *The Late Show with David Letterman.*

It was great to say hello to Rob Burnett.

A couple of weeks prior to our conversation, I received a call from a publicist saying that Rob would like to come on the show to talk about his film *The Fundamentals of Caring*, starring Paul Rudd, Craig Roberts, and Selena Gomez, which was premiered on Netflix. I was happy to book Rob on the show and chat about the film, but I relished the chance to also discuss his time working with and for David Letterman.

We began by talking about *The Fundamentals of Caring*, which Rob produced, wrote, and directed. I could hear the pride in Rob's voice as he talked about this film, *his* film. The plot revolves around two men, each dealing with severe limitations, one physical, the other emotional, and their journey to help and eventually inspire each other. Burnett's trademark is comedy, and he positions the film where it avoids sentimental cliches and instead reaches for tasteful laughs.

Paul Rudd, one of the male leads, has evolved into a dependable Hollywood star, and Rob truly wanted Rudd to be a part of the film: "Rob, I've heard you say that you were dreaming of Paul Rudd as you were writing the script as if he would be perfect for this, and he's also a very accomplished writer. So how did that add to the creative element within himself and his own performance in the film?"

Ed, I'll tell you, it's great to have Paul in your movie for a million reasons. Yes, you get what you get on screen, which is incredible. But he's also just a great guy to have around on set. He always had great notes on the script. It was just another person there who would see things the way I would want them to be seen, but with a fresh eye so he could say, 'Hey, maybe let's not do this. Let's do this instead.' And so, he was a huge help from top to bottom. Honestly, if I was doing another movie and I couldn't get Paul Rudd to star in it, I'd love to have him as a producer, I would do that in a second. He's a very talented man.

I then wondered about Rob Burnett's filmmaking process. As the producer, director, and writer and considering the creativity of the cast, did the script change much once on set from what Rob originally wanted to do?

It didn't change very much at all. Although, as I recall, there was a scene in The Fundamentals of Caring where I did allow the actors to stray from the script. In it, Paul's character is trying to get Craig's character to try a Slim-Jim for the first time and Paul ad-libs almost the entire exchange. It was hilarious, and it turned out to be wonderful work.

"Rob, it's nice when you have an atmosphere like that to kind of explore things and improvise a little bit. Look at what Larry David did with *Curb Your Enthusiasm.*"

Exactly right, Ed.

"Rob, I've acted in a couple of smaller films where if you deviate one syllable from the written word, all hell breaks loose, so it must be so great and refreshing to be able to have an environment where you can tell an actor that's it's OK to go ahead and see what they can do with a situation."

It all comes down to the individual actor, honestly. You know what I mean? There's nothing worse in life than bad improv. But, if you've got Paul Rudd in your movie, you'd kind of be an idiot to not let him do his stuff.

I wanted to pivot to Rob's long association with David Letterman, but I needed an artful way in which to make such a delicate transition. Hmm, I needed to blend Rob's new film somehow with Dave. Here goes...

"You know, considering what you've done for the past couple of decades, it begs the question, did Dave Letterman call you at any point and say, 'uh, Rob, if you happen to need a guy with a pretty long beard at this point, I could be at the airport in an hour.' "

Rob laughed out loud and then told me: *I can tell you with one hundred percent certainty that I did not get that call. I was called neither by Dave nor his beard for this film.*

Mission accomplished. Even if I do say so myself, that transition was as artful as Bob Ross painting a tree using only the side of a butter knife and an eyelash brush. The door was now open, let's talk about Letterman.

Rob Burnett enjoyed a long association with David Letterman, an association which began in 1985 when Rob became an intern on NBC's *Late Night with David Letterman*. He evolved to head writer, moved with Letterman to CBS, and eventually became the long-time executive producer of *The Late Show*. Burnett joined Letterman at a very interesting time. Letterman was in the process of morphing from David into "Dave." The first couple of years of *Late Night* showed a Letterman, who was a tad more reserved, more of a traditional broadcaster than an entertainer, someone who seemed like a traffic cop guiding the more modern and seemingly experimental comedy being provided by bit players and the staff. It was Letterman at his "aw shucks" somewhat couched midwestern best. Around '85 or '86, though, the audience began to see more of "Dave." Dave had a much more expressive and loud approach, with curlier grown-out hair, the trademark cigar often in hand, the flamboyant 1980s sneakers with the suit, and a personality more suited to the material around him and the audience that he pursued. Considering that Burnett stayed with Letterman for almost three decades, it's hard to imagine that Rob wasn't an integral part of that pretty obvious metamorphosis.

Late-night television is a demanding animal. It's a five-night-a-week grind to create five hours of live-to-play television, and that five-night-a-week grind is really five very long days that begin early in the morning and continue at a breakneck pace until the taping begins at 5:30 PM. Then, one additional hour to create a compelling and entertaining product right up until 6:30 PM when the host waves and says, "Goodnight, everybody!" That must create a great deal of pressure.

You do have a lot of pressure. The difference in doing late night as opposed to a film, I think, is that the Late Show was much more disposable. You know, you're doing five of them a week, and they can only be so good just by the nature of what they are. With the Late Show, it just felt like you were running around doing the best you can. It's a sprint, and then 5:30 comes, and it's time to tape, and whatever you get, you gotta go with it.

Listening to Rob describe that frenetic atmosphere and calling the show disposable led to an obvious question. "Do you miss that job?"

Ed, I don't at the moment. Honestly, I'm still waiting for the great mourning to come, but I just think I had done it so long, and I do think, to some extent, maybe we may have stayed there a little bit longer than we should have.

When I heard Rob say that, I was a bit shocked. Here was David Letterman's executive producer, a man who was with him from the NBC nights at 12:30 and then into and through the CBS nights at 11:30, telling me, "*Maybe we may have stayed there a little bit longer than we should have.*" It is true that late-night television changed dramatically and was fragmented during Letterman's run. It is also true that Letterman himself changed during that run. Letterman tempered his act to create more mass appeal when he moved to 11:30, and as time progressed, the adventurous comedy bits were less frequent, and as Dave got older, the overall energy level of the show began to wane a bit. Meanwhile, Jimmy Fallon was now literally jumping up and down while singing with Justin Timberlake only a few blocks away on NBC. All of a sudden, the Top Ten Lists seemed a bit archaic, and the show started to become a bit dated. But to hear the executive producer admit that maybe they overstayed their welcome was quite telling.

"Why, Rob?"

Ed, I think a lot of the stuff that I loved about the show by the end was already gone, you know what I mean? Again, to be clear, it's stored in a very beautiful, nostalgic place in my brain. I'm very grateful for the opportunity of working at the Letterman show and, you know, that's an experience that I think very few people will ever have. That's old-time show business. You're in the Ed Sullivan Theater. You're running around. Where are the costumes? Where are the guests?

"Uh oh, Regis is five minutes late again, damn him," I said, almost trying to lighten Rob's mood, and thankfully, Rob immediately let out a loud laugh. He then said something ridiculously poignant that truly summed up how he felt now that his Letterman days were firmly in his rearview mirror.

I wouldn't trade it for the world, and I don't think I would do it again for the world, either.

At this point, after hearing that Rob believed the construct of the Letterman show had become a tad "old-time show business" and that a new era in late-night television had begun, I figured he was the perfect person to assess the situation.

"Rob, what are your feelings about the state of late-night television now as a genre? It's much more political, and it's going places where entertainment, and I say 'entertainment' with air quotes, has never really seemed to go before. How do you feel about where late night is today?"

Well, to be honest with you, I think late-night has never been better. I'm looking at these guys. I don't pore over it, but everybody's working really hard now, and I think this comes from competition. Look at Fallon, every night, they're doing stuff. Colbert as well, all of these guys. I think the main difference of late-night television from what it used to be way back is that in the old days, when you watched the Carson show, you watched that show because you wanted to spend an hour with Johnny. I think with Dave it was similar, but now it's all about the highlights. It's all about what click we can get on YouTube.

I then asked Rob if that made the overall product worse and if that added even more pressure in creating the show. Rob offered that it's not necessarily worse, it's just different.

The pressure is to create these viral highlights as opposed to, I want to sit down and spend an hour with this guy if that makes sense. I think that has reshaped things to some extent, and I think one of the differences you're seeing is that guys like Letterman and Jon Stewart, even to some extent, are guys that kind of sit back and make fun of things, whereas guys like Fallon, James Corden when he did it, and even Colbert to an extent are in the front of the room doing stuff. And I think in today's world, there's a real premium on performance. Do you know what I mean? Because you can create your own highlights. For us, in the later years of the show, it often came down to sitting there and waiting until Joaquin Phoenix went nuts on our show.

Right then, it hit me. Perhaps David Letterman came along too soon. It's an easy argument to make that many of Letterman's bits from the NBC days and in the very early CBS days, such as dropping old TVs and watermelons from buildings, Stupid Pet Tricks, Viewer Mail, and many of the out-of-studio segments, were quite ahead of their time and would have made great and most likely viral YouTube and social media moments if they aired today. Rob agreed.

Yes, I think in the old days when we were running around with cameras and Dave was working the Taco Bell drive-through and doing this and doing that, I think had the world been different back then, those clips would've gone viral.

I then mentioned my favorite out-of-studio Letterman production piece. It aired during the first week of the CBS show in the summer of 1993 and showed Dave driving around Manhattan and calling in ridiculous traffic tips to a New York radio station which featured, and still does, by the way, incredibly long traffic reports every ten minutes. It was something like: "Uh, is this WINS? Just wanna let you know there's about a five-car backup on Seventh Avenue because the light's red. You'd better get that on the air. Oops, wait a minute. Yup, the delay's clearing up, and the light's now green. Never mind."

Rob immediately started to laugh, and I realized I had just made two hot wires touch somewhere deep within the Letterman memory lobe inside his brain.

That's so funny that you're mentioning that. That piece was one of my favorites that we'd ever done. It was called "Fun with a Car Phone." That's when car phones weren't all that interesting. It was us driving around the city and we were in this little sports car. I remember this day like it was yesterday. It was 110 degrees out, and I was cramped in the back seat of that car in a fetal position with an audio guy. Dave was in the car, he was smoking cigars, and the top was down, and I literally thought I was going to die on this day. I was trying to decide what my obituary would say if I were to die in the back of this car. But I have to say, that was one of my favorite pieces ever. Dave was so funny in that.

"Now today," I warned my listeners, "when you see Rob sucking on an inhaler every 37 seconds, you'll know why."

Exactly, said Rob through a long giggle.

Our time had come to a close. I thanked him for being on the show and for his frank and open comments about the ending of the *Late Show*. I found Rob Burnett to be a man who wasn't living in the past or off previous laurels. He's a creative and forward-thinking guy who gave me the impression he can look in his personal rearview mirror and smile, while realizing it's more important and much more fun to look straight ahead through the windshield. What comes next is always more important. Maybe that's why the windshield is fifty times bigger than the rearview mirror.

And it also makes it easier to call in fake traffic reports to WINS.

22

Doug Momary and Emily Peden

Doug and Emmy Jo from the 1970s children's show *New Zoo Revue*

Children's minds and hearts are just like sponges. Everything they see, everything that is told to them is absorbed like a little sponge.

***

I opened an email and discovered a time machine. It was a busy morning where I had sort of let my email get ahead of me. I sat down in the studio and saw I had 17 unread messages. Uh oh, I better read them. No, I don't want new windows, even if I get a free storm door. I already have life insurance with your company. Ugh, they want me to congratulate someone on LinkedIn because they've been able to keep a job for two years. Ooh, here's one from the airline I always fly: buy 100,000 miles right now and get a free hard-boiled egg the next time I visit the Sky Club before my flight. Uh, I don't think so. Here's one from Danny, the Los Angeles-based publicist who has provided me with some very interesting guests over the years. What's up with, Danny?

I read Danny's email, and all of a sudden, I found myself transported back to a different time. In my mind, I was sitting on the forest green rug in front of our 25-inch Zenith TV. The time-appropriate wooden cabinet that housed the rounded rectangular screen was a bit gored on its lower right corner as my ability to drive my Big Wheel was hampered by my inability to negotiate that tight left turn just after the circular coffee table and just before the TV. Even though my physicality was firmly planted in my studio in September 2023, my thoughts and my spirit drifted back to 1973 and that second-floor apartment at the corner of West 4th Street and Trask Avenue in Bayonne, NJ. If you're keeping score in all of this, I lived as an infant in Jersey City, but we lived in Bayonne until the summer of '74, when I was seven and moved out to the suburbs of Edison.

What could be in this email that would instantly make me wax both poetic and nostalgic? Two names: Doug and Emmy Jo. One show: *New Zoo Revue.*

Oh my God! I could have Doug and Emmy Jo on my show. I'm sorry, but how friggin' cool is that? I realized that what I had just experienced with such a palpable and instantaneous trip into the deepest aisle of my mind's memory warehouse would most likely happen for others as well. I responded to Danny and agreed to the guest booking quicker than you can say, "Henrietta Hippo." Two weeks later, the studio phone rang.

It was great to say hello to Doug Momary and Emily Peden.

First, though, a bit of literary housekeeping: On the show, as anyone who ever watched it knows, Emily was Emmy Jo. Thus, I was faced with an internal struggle between the six-year-old me who watched the show back then and the much older than six-year-old me who was having a conversation on his radio show now. In the spirit of both consistency and maturity, I decided that for the ensuing conversation, I would refer to Emmy Jo as Emily.

I told Doug and Emily right off the bat that for the past two weeks, ever since I learned they were coming on the show, I couldn't get the show's theme song out of my mind. It had gotten to the point where it had invaded my everyday life.

"Doug and Emily, I have to tell you, just yesterday, I'm scanning groceries at the self-checkout, and I caught myself under my breath singing. 'It's the *New Zoo Revue,* coming right at you.' I think more than anything it proves I grew up with your show, does it not?"

Doug and Emily both chuckled, and then Doug said: *Yes, that makes me feel so good. We've been to several appearances and conventions, and people just still remember that song, and when, as an artist, when I'm sitting there composing it, you don't know it's going to last for 50 years and be a part of people's lives. So, I'm just so thankful and thrilled.*

"I understand; there you are back in the early '70s with your guitar and a pencil, writing the theme song; how could you know that some guy more than a half-century later would be singing it while bagging his English muffins?"

I then did a character reset for the listeners, almost as if to reach back into their mental treasure chests and rekindle memories of their own childhoods. There was Doug and Emmy Jo, along with Freddie the Frog, Charlie the Owl, and Henrietta Hippo, with a few other human friends. The show looked like the 1970s, but in a wonderful and appropriate way, with a bright and colorful set that was inviting and inspired imagination.

Doug and Emily were enjoying a *New Zoo Revue* renaissance when they appeared on the show, a renaissance which can be credited to their daughter. Yes, Doug and Emmy Jo are married and were so back when the show aired. Anyway, like many things today, it was social media that created a wave of renewed interest in the show.

Well, Ed, Joanna is our oldest daughter, Emily began, *and she said, "Mom and Dad, I think you have millions of people who love you, and you should make a Facebook page." She started it right there and it's just taken off. We've got over 46,000 followers and more every day. And our life has changed dramatically since that time. We're just having a blast meeting children who are grown up, who are your age now, that enjoyed our show when they were little.*

That Facebook page soon ended up hosting a Facebook Live session which was a major success. So much so, that it led to a booth at a Comic-Con in San Diego. The reaction of attendees, in many cases, was striking. It's quite a feeling to see a part of your childhood sitting at a table right in front of you.

"Emily, is it true that some fans even cried when they saw the two of you there?"

That is true. I think that's been a remarkable thing for us because when we did the show, we had no idea that it was actually impacting people's lives. Ed, as you just said, we had some people coming up in tears, and one gentleman said that his mother had passed away, and he remembered always watching the show sitting on his mama's lap. We also had people come and talk about how they had been very, very ill as children, and our show was a comfort to them. We could write a book right now with the stories that we've heard from people who were little kids enjoying our show, and it really did have an impact and we didn't know it. So this has been amazing for us and very, very rewarding. I will just say that we love our New Zoo kids. We love meeting them and we are just having so much fun with this great adventure that Joanna has started.

As Emily talked about these intense and almost visceral reactions, my mind brought me back to something I heard Emily read during one of their social media get-togethers I watched to prepare for our conversation. I reached for my notebook and thumbed to the page where I had my *New Zoo Revue* notes. I had written something that really struck me. I had to read it for Doug and Emily.

"I saw something from your Facebook Live, which now is also on YouTube, and it both struck me and moved me. Please allow me to take a moment and read it here."

Sure, said Emily, *please do.*

"My family fell apart when I was six. Watching the *New Zoo Revue* each morning was my happy place. My memories of the show are bittersweet because of the chaos around me at the time. But the respite it brought me, it probably saved me emotionally."

"That is so powerful," I continued. "It is so meaningful, and I think it underscores not only the popularity that *New Zoo Revue* had at the time and still does, but it underscores the tremendous and almost wonderful responsibility that the two of you and everyone involved in making that show had to the children who were watching every day. You are hearing the difference that the show made and continues to make in people. I just find that responsibility not daunting, but I find it quite amazing. Doug, what were you trying to accomplish with the show at the time?"

I'll tell you, we did want to have an impact. I can tell you that now because the other shows at that time were A-B-C *and* 1-2-3, *and Emily and I wanted to do a show that touched people's hearts about how you relate to your mom, your dad, your sister, and how to treat people kindly with love and respect. And when I was writing those songs, yes, I was hoping they would have an impact.*

Emily then talked about what's really fun for them. It's finding out what the kids who watched the show back then are doing today. She said many of them told her they are already grandparents. Some work in law enforcement, others are educators, IT professionals, entertainers, and many other fields. Emily then wondered if some of the adults who visited their table in San Diego were some of the same people they saw as kids at some personal appearance across Southern California back in the '70s. That's actually a bit mind-blowing if true.

I then pivoted to how children are quite impressionable and what they are exposed to is not only important but crucial. *New Zoo Revue* addressed the deeper educational needs of children and filled those needs responsibly. Emily agreed and then amplified my thoughts in a very prideful tone.

Children's minds and hearts are just like sponges, said Emily. *Everything they see, everything that is told to them, is absorbed like a little sponge. And that's why it's so important for parents and teachers and grandparents to be mindful of that when we are interacting with children.*

I reminded Doug what he mentioned a bit earlier when he said that other shows were concerned primarily with the basics: the A-B-Cs and the 1-2-3s, and obviously, they are important, but *New Zoo Revue* was different, and I sensed it was different, even when I was young sitting on that forest green rug.

"Doug, when the show first ran, it was when I was between the ages of five and ten, and even then, I knew your show was different from the other shows I watched. You talked about feelings, and you talked about emotions. You told me it was okay to feel however I was feeling, and it was a wonderful way for children to experience entertainment, which taught them understanding and about the feelings that are inside them and that they carry with them for the rest of their lives."

Think about this, Doug responded. *In order to do that, you had to establish characters that were identifiable. That's why in the other shows they quick cut things, two second clips, five seconds. We told a story with a beginning, a middle, and an end. It was a musical for kids that had a moral lesson at the end: tell the truth, treat people kindly. And I think kids followed that story and followed those characters in what we were telling them. We weren't talking down to them. I didn't want to preach. I didn't want to talk down to kids. I wanted to communicate with them on their level.*

"It didn't turn into a caricature of what a children's show should be," I replied.

Many of the other children's shows during that period, which had costumed or puppet characters, showed them as being quite small and sometimes unrealistically so. You never saw their legs, and you could never grasp a full image, but New Zoo Revue had characters that were full-dimensional. Freddie, Charlie, and Henrietta all walked around, they displayed regular movements, had their own human-like personalities, and expressed their own feelings. I asked Doug how important it was for those characters to possess that rich level of texture and personality.

It was extremely important, stressed Doug, *because in one of the episodes, Freddy the Frog sang a song called "It's Lonely When You Don't Like School." He was alone in the courtyard singing this song, and he had to be able to move and be sad, then be happy, and then be sad with all those emotions playing in that song. Each episode had those elements, so we had to show them with those human qualities. So, a kid could say, I felt that. I know that feeling.*

What's really funny, as Emily jumped in, *is that one of our New Zoo kids wrote on our Facebook page that she thinks Doug should write a new version of "It's Lonely When You Don't Like School." She said he should write "It's Lonely When You Don't Like Work."*

We all chuckled. Obviously, the *New Zoo* kids grew up with a pretty good sense of humor.

Ed, it's amazing to me, said Doug, *that the themes that I came up with back then are still viable today. They still speak to kids today. We tried to make these themes universal, and I think we did.*

As I prepared for our conversation, I also watched a few *New Zoo Revue* episodes, and I was quickly reminded of the show's sly and fun sense of humor.

"Doug and Emily, last night I watched your episode about eating. I wasn't expecting to laugh out loud, but all of a sudden, Charlie says, 'I once knew a girl who ate nothing but salads. She did it to keep trim. She ate salads for breakfast, salads for lunch, salads for dinner. She did it all the time.' Emmy Jo then asks, 'Did she end up trim and lovely?' Charlie replies, 'No, she ended up green and leafy.' I started cracking up. Here I am in my mid-fifties, and I'm watching a children's show that I first watched 50 years ago. It still makes me laugh now. It makes me recall something Carol Burnett told me a few years ago, that it's wonderful when a child and a parent and a grandparent can all get it and laugh together and share in the experience. You both accomplished that with this show. That is a wonderful thing."

Well, thank you, Doug said with appreciation. *We did put lines in there for parents. I wrote things, and actually, Charlie the Owl came up with a lot of ad-libs that went right over the kids' heads, but if you watch them now, you will be on the floor laughing. Many times, we needed to stop production back then because I was laughing.*

I then had to confirm something I read about the cast. Mr. Dingle, the friendly postman during the first season, was played by Chuck Woolery. Yes, that Chuck Woolery, the first host of *Wheel of Fortune*. Was this true?

Absolutely, exclaimed Emily, *and it was so fun to see where his career took him after* New Zoo Revue.

We gave him his first acting gig, said Doug.

"Wow, there never would've been Chuck sitting on the couch on *Love Connection* saying 'We'll be back in two and two' if not for his start as Mr. Dingle," I said somewhat nostalgically while realizing that I'll never again think of Chuck Woolery in the same way. Doug then commented how he and Chuck are about the same age, and here was Woolery back when he was in his thirties, playing a much older guy and pulling it off rather well.

As the show grew in popularity, it reached a point where it attracted a myriad of guest stars, including Henry Mancini, Jim Backus, Jesse White, June Lockhart, and even Richard Dawson of *Family Feud* fame.

How about Joanne Worley and Pat Paulsen? said Doug, adding to the list. *Having Henry Mancini on was great, and it was a fascinating process and so meaningful because, just think of this: I'm a young composer. I'm sitting in Freddy's rowboat on the pond and talking to Henry Mancini, and so I asked him off camera, "Hey, can you give me some advice about composing?" He said, "Yeah, just keep writing."*

"That's simple but right to the point, Doug," I said, confirming my status as Captain Obvious. Doug wrote over 600 original songs for the show, and it's daunting to think about the logistics of creating even just one thirty-minute episode, including the choreography, the blocking, and the setting of cameras and lights. It's an incredible amount of work, but it also must have been quite a labor of love.

It was a labor of love, said Emily, *but it was so much fun. We enjoyed it so much. I remember long hours. I remember getting up really, really, really early in the morning, but I don't remember it being something that was hard because our cast was so wonderful. All the people that worked on the show were like a family, and it was just a great experience from beginning to end.*

Well, Ed, first we had to write the shows, explained Doug. *It was a process which began before we even started the first season, and as you mentioned I composed all the music. We had to go in every week and pre-record an entire album of songs. There were three original songs in each episode, and each song, as in a musical comedy, had to further the plot. And so, I came up with the storylines. We had a talented group of staff writers who would put some flesh onto the story, and then we would rehearse two shows on Monday and tape those two shows on Tuesday, do the same thing on Wednesday, tape those two shows on Thursday, and then on Friday, we would pre-record the next week's album. All of this was done without syncing; everything was done live. We cut the musical numbers live, three cameras cut live, and they did very little touch-up in the editing because it was all on a two-inch videotape.*

Wow, I became tired just listening to that workload. But when you go back and watch an episode, you can easily see both the meticulous care and herculean effort which went into producing the show. Add to that the fact that it was a much different time in television when creating consistently excellent programming such as *New Zoo Revue* was much more difficult and challenging than it is today.

What helped the show reach an average viewership of at least three million people a day was the fact it was broadcast nationally in first-run syndication. Remember, this was before cable TV; during the early to mid-1970s, there were usually only five or six commercial channels on the air in any given market.

"When I was growing up in Northern New Jersey, Doug and Emily, you were on at a wonderful time. The show was broadcast on WPIX Channel 11, which was one of the big independent stations in New York City, and for most of the show's original run, you were on at 1:30 in the afternoon. If you were a kid at home during the summer, if you were home sick, or if you were of preschool age, there was nothing else at that time for a child to watch because everything else was either a game show or a soap opera. The show originally ran in first-run syndication from '72 to '77 but continued in reruns for years after that. Doug, how important was the fact that you had first-run syndication and you were in all of these markets in these wonderful positions in the afternoon schedule? That truly expanded the scope of the show, did it not?"

It really did, and we were able to grow the show in popularity. I mean, we were invited to the White House two times!

"Wow, I never knew that!"

We did the Easter Egg Roll, said Doug. *This was back in the Nixon years when we brought all the characters with us and did a live show, and we also did a show for the children of foreign diplomats that Mrs. Nixon hosted one Christmas.*

I couldn't resist: "Did you ever find out which character was Richard Nixon's favorite?"

"No," replied Doug, "he never showed up."

Damn. We'll never know if it was Freddy, Charlie, or Henrietta. Maybe somewhere on one of those tapes, well, never mind. I then brought up the importance of *New Zoo Revue* even today and told Doug and Emily that the world in which we live in today is one which needs the show's themes and lessons more than ever.

Ed, I think you're absolutely right, said Doug. *When I look at television for kids now, it has turned dark, in my opinion, and I don't like that. I think that we need messages of hope and kindness and tolerance, and you don't see that very often.*

Doug and Emily's reemergence on social media and now through live events and appearances has rekindled relationships with viewers, which began when these viewers were in their single digits and are now firmly planted in middle age. This reattached connection has people divulging all kinds of information to Doug and Emily.

Ed, we know what most of you had for breakfast, said Emily. *A lot of you are writing to us on social media and saying things like, "I remember I always had my Fruit Loops before I went to school while watching* New Zoo Revue*."*

Uh oh, at that point, my synapses began firing, and it was my turn to enter the *New Zoo Revue* confessional.

"Doug and Emily, hearing your voices is taking me back, as we speak, to the middle of 1973 and *my* favorite cereal. I would be sitting and watching the two of you while eating a bowl of Quisp. I loved Quisp, and then one day it was gone. It had just disappeared and was gone for so long. Then, one day, about ten years ago, there it was. It was back, albeit for a limited time only. I stumbled upon it in a supermarket, and it was my Doug and Emmy Joe at Comic-Con moment. I teared up. I said to myself, 'It's Quisp. It really is Quisp.' I took it home. I devoured three bowls of it, and then the next day, my teeth hurt like they'd never hurt before in my entire life. So, you know what? Some things are left back in the past except, of course, for *New Zoo Revue*."

Doug and Emily both let out a hearty laugh. It was the perfect way to wrap up our conversation, one which I very much enjoyed. My personal trip back to my childhood was a fun one. We said our goodbyes, and off went Doug and Emmy Jo to enjoy the rest of their day.

Later that afternoon, I received a call from my dentist to schedule when I could come in to have the permanent crown installed after my recent root canal.

That damn Quisp.

23

Todd Rundgren

Musician, Singer, Songwriter, and Record Producer

A musician is supposed to continue to evolve not only for himself but for the benefit of the audience so that they don't become stuck in some musical backwater somewhere.

***

There are artists in various fields of performance that transcend their art and their industry. They become legendary not only to their audience but to their fellow performers as well. They tend to push their industries to stretch boundaries and explore new ways to express their talent. It is always incredibly exciting to have the opportunity to talk with such an artist.

It was great to say hello to Todd Rundgren.

As I drove up to the studio the morning I was scheduled to record my conversation with Todd, I was streaming much of the Rundgren catalog through my car's Bluetooth. I've always believed the true go-to Todd Rundgren song is 1972's "Hello It's Me." It has that prototypical "singers and songwriters" sound to it, which was so prevalent during the early '70s. But as I continued to listen to more and more Rundgren during a traffic-laden hour-long ride that drizzly morning, I found myself venturing aurally into the more esoteric side of Todd Rundgren, especially his 1974 album, *Todd Rundgren's Utopia.* While songs such as "Hello It's Me" and "I Saw the Light" were heard on all the major AM Top 40 stations, *Utopia* showed a side of Rundgren much better suited for the FM audience of its day. It was more experimental and allowed Rundgren the outlet to let his music become his own artistic laboratory.

The ever-evolving career and sound of Todd Rundgren had brought him to his latest multimedia release, *An Evening with Todd Rundgren - Live at the Ridgefield.* Todd was booked on the show to talk about it and to chat about a career that could be considered incredibly eclectic. This new release, though, was a chance to look back at fan-favorite performances, albeit through a modern prism. Looking back is something Todd doesn't do all that often.

Well, Ed, essentially, I don't do this kind of thing as a habit. When I have new music that I've made and continue to make new music, most of my shows are based around that new music. The fans will respond to it in the way that they usually do, which is positive or negative, but they usually give me the benefit of the doubt, which is great. But after time, it sometimes seems like I'm refusing to play the things that they want to hear. So, I decided before I make the next big leap, I'm going to touch base with my fans. I'm gonna do the songs that, in their heart of hearts, they've been yelling for. So, what I tried to do here is make a show that essentially was all the requests and play it in a way that they remember it instead of rearranging it to something more contemporary or different, as they want to kind of go back in their minds to when they first heard these songs. You know, with the girlfriend they had or the situation they were in when they first heard the song.

Todd has always evolved with the times and technology. As the music industry changed, he changed with it. But music fans are nostalgic by nature, especially as they grow older. So, for an artist like

Rundgren, who always moved forward, he needed to balance that with a fanbase always yearning to look back. That cannot be easy.

"Todd, that's quite a weird dichotomy, isn't it?"

Well, I established that dynamic pretty early on in my career. My third album was the most commercially successful because it had "I Saw the Light," "Hello It's Me," and one or two other minor hits on it. And after I put that album out, everyone thought I was going to try and capitalize on it and continue to do the same thing. Instead, I went off on a completely different tangent with an album called A Wizard, a True Star, *in which I kind of deconstructed song structure and tried to imprint on the record all of the crazy influences that I had musically. It kind of lopped off about half my fan base right off the bat. The people who did stay, you know, realized that maybe this is going to turn out to have a little bit more of an interesting storyline rather than me doing the same thing over and over after that.*

I learned during our conversation that Todd is a big fan of The Beatles. He attributes that to his own desire not to do the same things over and over. Todd was eager to illustrate both his admiration of the Fab Four and the influence they had on him.

Ed, people forget how often The Beatles changed genres. There was no such thing as classical rock until "Eleanor Rigby," and then there was no such thing as psychedelic rock until "Strawberry Fields Forever." They would do these things, and then they would move on, and I thought that's what a musician is supposed to do. A musician is supposed to continue to evolve not only for himself but for the benefit of the audience so that they don't become stuck in some musical backwater somewhere and don't realize all of the great possibilities that are out there.

When you do a deep dive into the works of Todd Rundgren, you can definitely sense a Beatles influence. But I wanted to cast a larger net and learn more about who and what influenced Todd.

"You developed during an amazing time in music: the mid-'60s, music was changing. Other than The Beatles, who were some of your biggest influences?

Like you say, it was an amazing time. It had to do with radio because, during that time, radio was very local and also personality-based. The DJs really were just jockeys in the literal sense, and they could decide, while one record was playing, which record to play next instead of going off of some big list of records given to them. As radio became more successful, just as music became more successful, it became more and more structured. But I was lucky enough to grow up in an era when DJs were competing with each other for what kind of music they could get on the radio.

Todd had just struck a chord within me. If you know anything about me, you know the influence that radio, especially music radio, had on me during pretty much the same time Todd just referenced. Although I was more of a fan of structured Top 40 AM radio, such as what was heard in my neck of the woods on WABC in New York, as well as what was being done in Los Angeles on KHJ, Todd is correct about it being an age of freedom and expression for DJs, especially for those who worked on the progressive FM stations. In many markets, these FM stations were still searching for commercial viability. The AMs made the money, while the FMs were properties that were allowed to find their own way and be discovered by an audience. Thus, eclectic programming ruled early FM radio, and even as early as the late '60s and early '70s, people began to migrate from predictable AM formats to the more explorative ones being presented on FM. Todd hammered my point home.

A typical radio show back then on FM might be like The Beatles, then you'd hear Bob Dylan, then you might hear Bill Evans or another jazz artist of some kind, then even a folk artist. It was sort of all mixed up, and the audience was incredibly open to whatever it was that the DJ would play. And that even extended to live shows. You would see shows that just had the most unlikely combination of artists, so even if you came to see a particular person, you would get exposed to other kinds of music.

Todd and I went on to discuss how the music industry is no longer nearly as organic as it was. He feels we've gone from a time when music, artists, and songs in particular, earned its popularity from people actually hearing it to today, where the industry and its product are driven more by pre-release hype and publicity.

Maybe the most unfortunate thing about music nowadays is that we don't have the same kind of liberated arbiters who can go out and listen to all the music there is and try and pick the best of it and play it for everyone. Everything is a bit publicity-driven now. You hear about things before you actually hear them. It used to be the other way around. You would hear something on the radio, and you'd say, "What is that?" And then you'd try and find out about it. Now you hear about something that you haven't heard and maybe won't ever hear again because the next day it's something else.

"It seems you're telling me that music has become very disposable. It is true that there's so much of it now because there are so many platforms from which new music drops. Is that a good or a bad thing? Is there too much music at this point?"

Well, Ed, I suppose the politically correct answer would be there's never enough music.

"What's the real answer?"

Okay, well, the real answer is you can't force people to listen to music the way you want them to listen to it. They're always going to listen to it the way they want, and if music is simply a fashion or a lifestyle accessory to them, so be it. Maybe in one sense, it always was; maybe in one sense, the audience never got down to the level that the artist wanted them to.

At this point, the clock on the wall said it was time to begin to put a bow on my conversation with Todd Rundgren, but I needed to extract one more nugget. What was the perfect finish? "Todd, tell me about the coolest thing that ever happened to you on stage."

Oh wow, here's what happened to me a very long time ago when I was mostly record producing and I was a solo artist. I was working for the Albert Grossman organization and I was hanging out with all the biggest stars in the world. These bands were the hottest thing happening at the time. So, I got invited to a lot of events, and one of those events was Eric Clapton headlining at Madison Square Garden. Eric Clapton was my idol. Before I ever wrote a song, I wanted to be a guitar player, like Eric Clapton, and I thought if I couldn't, I would throw myself in the river. Fortunately, things had evolved to that point where Eric Clapton, you know, he and I could actually be considered on almost on the same level. I could have a conversation with him, and he invited me to jam with him at Madison Square Garden, which, first of all, made me poop my pants. This is the very idea of wow. I went out there, and the very first thing I did was break a string, almost on the first note that I had. I broke a string, and Eric Clapton handed me his guitar.

"Whoa, oh my God."

Eric Clapton handed me his guitar to finish my solo! It's the coolest thing that ever happened to me on stage.

Mic drop. Todd had just taken his figurative guitar and brought our time together to the perfect crescendo. I thanked Todd, and off he went to finish his day. I got the impression he truly enjoyed our conversation, as did I. I always enjoy speaking with a music artist whose work has contributed to the soundtrack of my own life.

That's why there's always room for music royalty on the show.

24

Dionne Warwick

Singer and Second-Most-Charted Female Vocalist During the Rock Era.

I was pretty, pretty fortunate in that I was in the right place at the right time.

***

Music is the soundtrack of our lives. It defines a time, a place, an experience. Music can evoke a range of emotions depending upon the memory it conjures at any precise moment. It lives in our hearts and our souls. Perhaps the most impactful aspect of music is the human voice, which can create true melodic art when blended with a thoughtful arrangement and perfect instrumentation. There are singers who possess a vocal fingerprint that instantly identifies them within our culture as exceedingly unique.

Over the years, I've spoken with many music artists, but few have created a catalog that bridges decades and generations and who are regarded as pivotal performers within their industry. It is a personal honor whenever I have the opportunity to speak with someone who has reached that summit.

It was great to say hello to Dionne Warwick.

Normally, the interviews for the show are recorded during the day, usually either late morning or early afternoon New York time. In this case, Dionne was in the middle of a very busy week and had asked if there was any way we could do the interview one evening after dinner. Yes, for true music royalty, it's quite easy for me to agree to go back down into the studio right after finishing off that evening's allotment of ground turkey meatloaf laced with diced tomatoes and onions.

The phone rang shortly before 7:30, I tapped the answer button: "Studio line, can I help you?"

Hi, Ed, it's Dionne Warwick. And off we went.

It was an interesting time to speak with Dionne as it was only a couple of months after the passing of legendary composer and songwriter Burt Bacharach. The media was full of Bacharach retrospectives, and most of them touched on his partnership with Dionne Warwick. However, this was Dionne's chance to talk with me and America about the working relationship she shared with Burt. We ended up talking about many things that evening.

Our conversation began with the music of Bacharach and Warwick. It is undeniable that there are very few collaborations in the history of American music that have worked as well and had the impact of Dionne Warwick, Burt Bacharach, and lyricist Hal David. I asked Dionne why she believed it worked so well.

We were known in the industry as a triangle marriage that worked, and it worked because we, first of all, had a wonderful friendship, and most importantly, they were writing wonderful songs for me to sing. When you have a collaboration with music that Burt wrote and the words that Hal had me sing, I don't think you can find anything better.

I told Dionne that for me, the most striking thing about the music conceived and produced by that triangle marriage is that all of those songs have a wonderful vein of substance that connects them. "Walk

On By," "I Say a Little Prayer," "Alfie," and many others are foundational columns in the American songbook of the second half of the 20th century. Each is distinct in its own way, but yet there is an unmistakable tone and feel which encompasses them all. I then asked Dionne if, at the time, it surprised her in any way that each of those songs were having the impact they did. Dionne said she believed it was because they were saying things that people wanted to hear and were melodies that were lasting melodies. Then she admitted something else.

I was pretty, pretty fortunate in that I was in the right place at the right time and fit very well into the duo who were writing these songs.

A few nights earlier, as I prepared for our conversation, I watched some of Dionne's appearances on *The Ed Sullivan Show*. That show was a staple of American entertainment during its run; for years, it was how America ended its weekend. Appearing on the show was continued validation for established stars and a springboard to stardom for new talent. As I watched, I tried to imagine what it must have been like to have that platform, that stage. It was a time when TV was channels 2 through 13, which meant CBS, NBC, ABC, and maybe an independent station or two if you happened to live in a large city. Being on television back then meant having quite a large part of the country watching you, and on the *Sullivan Show*, that meant watching you live.

"Dionne, you made several appearances on *The Ed Sullivan Show*, and there you were, a girl from New Jersey doing your thing in front of America. I have to ask, what was it like to have *that* stage, especially during *that* time in America?"

It was an absolutely incredible experience whenever I was invited to do the show, as it was The Ed Sullivan Show. *It was the show to be seen on and watched throughout the entire United States every Sunday night, and he was a wonderful man. It was a joy to do his show.*

Dionne agreed that it was truly appointment television as well as a uniting platform for America as Ed Sullivan himself was color blind.

He didn't see color, he saw talent and embraced Black performers in ways other shows of the time simply did not.

At the time we spoke, Dionne had also recently lost another close friend. Singer Chuck Jackson, who ironically was one of the first artists to record material by Burt Bacharach and Hal David and is best remembered for iconic late 1950s hits "Any Day Now" and "I Don't Want to Cry," passed away only eight days after Bacharach. Dionne and Chuck shared a very special relationship from a point very early in their careers. I sensed Dionne was still feeling the loss of Chuck quite hard.

Ed, Chuck happened to be a label mate. He was on a label called Wand. It was one of the labels that was a part of Scepter Records, which I was on. Chuck just fell into that 'big brother' realm; he just wanted to take very good care of me.

"Dionne, it sounds as if Chuck was extremely important to you," I said.

We still spoke every single day. He was a joy to know, an absolute joy, and when I heard he had passed, it hurt my heart because I lost what I considered a family member. Chuck was wonderful, and what a voice from the heavens, what a voice.

I was taken by how affected Dionne seemed by Chuck Jackson's passing. She was still obviously processing his loss, especially since he was someone she was speaking with every day until his death. I knew about Chuck Jackson and his own storied career, but I never knew of his close relationship with Dionne. It seemed to me Dionne wanted to talk about Chuck, so I continued: "Dionne, you worked with Chuck, and in 1998, the two of you recorded 'If I Let Myself Go.' Tell me what it was like to work with him."

It's a joy. When we're singing well, he with me and me with him, and I'm singing with someone with that exceptional voice. It's bringing me to my pinnacle as well. It was wonderful working with him.

The most important part of any conversation is not the ability to speak; it's the ability to listen. When I heard that last response from

Dionne, what struck me most was that she still talked about Chuck in the present tense until that last sentence. It's very hard for us to talk about people in the past tense who meant so much and who are now gone. We've all done that; it's one of the biggest hurdles to clear when we're dealing with loss. Dionne Warwick is a world-famous celebrity, but she is also human and deals with the same emotions we all do.

I continued talking about Chuck. "Dionne, for me, one of the things that always reinforces a music artist's legacy is how their work is perceived by other artists, and the number of covers of Chuck's work is incredibly impressive, artists such as Ronnie Milsap, Michael McDonald, David Bowie. Chuck was always so respected within the community and that'll never change."

Never, she emphasized. *Chuck earned every ounce of respect, and I'm so thrilled that you're reiterating that. He was very well respected within the industry.*

At this point of the conversation, I wanted to change the focus and look at what Dionne is doing now. There have been some wonderful partnerships in music: Lennon and McCartney, Simon and Garfunkel, Warwick and Bacharach. Now, there is another: Dionne Warwick and Dolly Parton. Two huge stars from different music genres but proving that talent can always work with talent. I asked Dionne about their recently released single "Peace Like a River."

Dolly sent me a song quite a few months ago, nothing related to "Peace Like a River," and I liked the song. I called Dolly and said this is a really good song, and when I get back to the studio, I intend to record it. She told me she had another song she wanted me to hear, and she sent me "Peace Like a River." I fell in love with it. I called Dolly again and said, you know, we have to do this together. So, I flew to Nashville, and we recorded and did the video.

Dionne Warwick and Dolly Parton working together in the same studio. "What is it like to work with Dolly?"

Dolly's wonderful. She's as funny as all get out; she should have been a comedian. I think we laughed more than anything. Dolly's really truly a wonderful lady.

I mentioned to Dionne that I'm also from New Jersey, so I know a little about where she grew up, and asked her about a special place near and dear to her heart. I asked her to tell me about a place on Central Avenue in East Orange: the Dionne Warwick Institute. Immediately, the listeners to our conversation could hear immense pride in Dionne's voice as told me that the Dionne Warwick Institute is the school she attended as a child, the former Lincoln School. The city of East Orange renamed the school in her honor about 10 or 12 years ago.

Ed, I cannot tell you enough how it is the accolade I will cherish for the rest of my life. It's something that will be here long after I'm gone, and knowing they considered me worthy of having my name on that particular building is sometimes overwhelming.

A few months prior to our conversation, the Dionne Warwick Institute was granted lighthouse status, an extremely prestigious recognition, and certification that a school has produced outstanding results in both school and student outcomes by implementing a process of fidelity and excellence. "Dionne," I said, "that's quite an achievement by the school."

Yes, it is, and I must give credit to the instructors there, and especially the principal of the school. They care so much about my babies, and they are my babies. It shows in the performance of these kids. They can't wait to get to school.

I was taken by how Dionne said not once but twice that the students are *her babies.* Here is a woman whose name and voice are recognized the world over by generations of people, yet what seemed to satisfy her the most when we spoke was a group of kids in East Orange, New Jersey. People often talk about giving back, and honestly, many celebrities do it in order to create self-gratifying social media posts and to simply look good. Dionne Warwick is way past that. It is the school she attended years before she had ever heard of Burt Bacharach or Hal David, knew Ed Sullivan, had gold records, and achieved superstardom. It is her history that she now sees serving children in her community. That must be an amazing feeling.

The kids tell me they can't wait to get to school. They say they get there early to say hello to their teachers before going to class. It's that kind of a school; it's almost a family affair.

"Dionne, it's a second home, and that's what school should be."

I agree totally, and I'm so happy my school has that ambiance.

We then pivoted to talking about Dionne's life on social media. She's made quite a name for herself on various platforms, but the one that caught my attention the most was her Facebook and Instagram series called *Nobody Asked for This*. I watched an episode the night before I spoke with Dionne and found it delightful. In it, Dionne told the story of running into Diahann Carroll in the grocery store, a story which had a couple of laugh-out-loud moments. I mentioned to Dionne how the series is such a great and intimate way to communicate with her fans. She agreed, saying people want to know more about her, some of the things she does now, and some of the things that have happened to her over the course of both her career and life. Most importantly, Dionne said she's finding it fun to do.

I love learning new things about guests during conversations. When I first learned that Dionne would be coming on the show, the last thing I thought we would be talking about is interior design. The 2020s version of Dionne Warwick is a woman who puts quite a great deal of time into her interior design company: WG Design Lab. Dionne's firm has done some incredibly attractive work. The night before we spoke, I had the chance to look at some photos detailing work done at the home of Ernest and Tova Borgnine in the Hollywood Hills, the Black Ensemble Theater in Chicago, and some others.

"What inspired you to pursue interior design?"

I think every little girl wants to be an interior designer in a way, wanting to change the color of the walls and change the color of the bedspread or the curtains. I find interior design really walks hand in hand with music and has all the same elements: warmth, coolness, and texture. All the things that music has, design has it, too.

That blew me away. I never thought of that. Music is art, interior design is art, it makes perfect sense. My time with Dionne was coming to a close, and I had to tell her what, for me, was the ironic part of having her on the show. Ironic that many times when I walk into my mother-in-law's kitchen, I hear Dionne's voice singing. My mother-in-law has a CD of all the biggest Burt Bacharach hits, many of them performed by Dionne. She plays it often.

"Dionne, you remain the soundtrack of so many days and so many lives, that has to be such an incredible feeling."

It's absolutely wonderful to know that people appreciate what I'm giving them, enjoy it, and want more of it, which is a wonderful thing.

I always find it fascinating how a performer, be it an actor, a host, or a singer, can create a cultural footprint that extends decades and generations. They remain relevant, and their work continues to be seen or heard, and it happens because the work they produced and created is still in demand, perhaps because of its nostalgic value, but primarily because it's just that good. Dionne Warwick is the perfect example. During our conversation, Dionne told me she was fortunate because she was in the right place at the right time. I think talent is immune to both place and time. Dionne still would have succeeded wherever and whenever she came along.

That's the definition of a true music genius.

Afterword

I've always absorbed media, literature, performance, and entertainment the way an overly porous sponge absorbs water.

***

I grew up during a great time. I was a child of the 1970s and the 1980s guided me from adolescence into young adulthood. It was a wonderful time to be entertained, a period in which we were all entertained as one. Even with the early influence of cable, television during that time was pretty much channels 2 through 13 and we watched shows together, on the same night and at the same time. It created a common link through pop culture which brought us closer. The only thing which approaches that now is Super Bowl Sunday. Today, there are hundreds of channels, dozens of streaming services, and countless shows which are simply "content." Entertainment and those who entertained us back in the day simply seemed bigger.

When I recall growing up, I think of time slots. Tuesday at 8pm meant *Happy Days* on ABC, followed by *Laverne & Shirley*. Friday at 8pm was *Sanford and Son* on NBC followed later at 9 by *The Rockford Files*. I knew the weekend was over and it was time to go to bed Sunday nights at 9pm when from the TV downstairs in the "rec room" (there's quite the '70s phrase) I heard the *Kojak* theme playing on CBS. I had no need for a hip new Casio digital watch because primetime television was my clock. But there was one night each week which stood out far more than any other.

Saturday nights on CBS between 1971 and 1978 was the gold standard of American television and, in turn, American pop culture. Shows such as *All in the Family, The Mary Tyler Moore Show, M*A*S*H, The Bob Newhart Show, The Jeffersons,* and *The Carol Burnett Show* quickly became appointment television and brought performers, characters, and personalities into the collective living room of America and helped define a decade. We laughed together and, whether we knew it at the time or not, began to see and understand a changing America. Norman Lear, creator most notably of *All in the Family* but also many other evolutionary sitcoms of that era, changed the purpose of the half hour situation comedy by holding a mirror up to our human psyche and allowed us to examine our societal thoughts, ideas, mores, and long held beliefs in ways that entertainment had never done. Lear made it ok to laugh and think at the same time and felt comfortable using the three-camera arrangement on a Hollywood soundstage as a societal prism.

When I had the pleasure of chatting with Norman on my radio show, he said he and his writers always had the goal of creating "a show (the audience) could watch and talk about afterwards." *M*A*S*H* was set in 1950s Korea but was making a very important statement through thoughtful comedy about America's involvement in Vietnam. Carol Burnett gave us the opportunity to sit with our families and laugh out loud together. The sketch comedy of *The Carol Burnett Show* with Carol, Tim Conway, and Harvey Korman holds up to this day as both hysterical and brilliant. *The Mary Tyler Moore Show* and *The Bob Newhart Show* showed us both an accurate and sophisticated look at our workplaces and adult friendships and relationships. Finally, television had grown up and the days of *Green Acres* were behind us. As someone watching from my childhood home in New Jersey, those 1970s Saturday nights on CBS always concluded with the 11pm local news on WCBS-TV in New York, anchored during much of that period by John Tesh. Yes, *that* John Tesh, the guy who years later was seen playing his piano at Red Rocks in Colorado during all those PBS fundraising specials.

We are quite fortunate that YouTube has become our modern-day instant time machine which allows people of all generations to go back and either relive or experience for the first time these wonderful shows which defined later mid-twentieth century television. Carol Burnett told me: *I'm getting fan mail from nine-year-olds, teenagers, and people in their twenties because funny is funny.* Nothing was funnier than the sketch comedy of *The Carol Burnett Show* and it remains hilarious to this day.

I was always intrigued by talk shows, on both radio and television, and my most impressionable years were flush with a number of great talents. I didn't just watch them, I tried to understand them. I tried to see what made each not just different but unique. Even though they all worked within the same basic premise and format, each tended to carve out their own true niche. Still, within the general conversation, one name always seems to come up first. Ask anyone within my chronological frame of reference and they usually begin with the same name: Johnny Carson.

Johnny Carson was sophistication personified. Every night: impeccably dressed, in total control, and at all times knowing the place he held in American culture. It took a bit of time to find itself after its debut in October of 1962, but once it got its footing, Johnny Carson's version of *The Tonight Show* on NBC found itself in a place perhaps no other show could even dream to reach. Carson's heyday existed before cable television and continued into cable's infancy and adolescence. There weren't many choices of quality television entertainment at 11:30pm in the 1960s, 1970s, and even much of the 1980s. Because of that, Johnny may have at first attracted his audience by default. But once he got them, he kept them. Carson's ability to allow a guest to shine was his best attribute. The chair next to Carson's desk was the goal of every actor, author, comedian, and compelling personality of the time. Johnny was perfect at what he did and for when he did it. Johnny was the comforting heated weighted blanket which ended America's collective day and allowed it to smile as it fell asleep. Carson was apolitical on the air and for him, that approach worked perfectly. He was everyone's comedian. Henry Bushkin, Carson's longtime attorney and confidant, appeared on my show and explained how Carson, off the air, was much different and had a less than perfect personal life. The slick, polished entertainer was in fact human. But on the air, Carson definitely earned his longtime moniker as the King of Late Night.

There were challengers to Carson's throne, none came close, but one managed to cross the moat, encroach the castle, and was able to hang out in the gift shop for a number of years. It was Dick Cavett. Cavett flawlessly combined the cerebral with the comedic, with both a remarkable respect of language and a sense of humor that could be biting yet always pitch perfect. *The Dick Cavett Show* on ABC in the early 1970s had a much different feel than Carson's *Tonight Show.* Cavett's was a simple set built for long form conversation, staged in an echoey Manhattan theater. As a writer for both Jack Paar and Johnny Carson in the early 1960s, Cavett understood late night television but took it a step further. His task was not to merely allow the most familiar faces of American culture to come on and do their thing, Cavett brilliantly allowed the viewer to learn more about these people. What made them tick? Why are they who they are? Cavett never brought questions with him, he brought curiosity, and that respectful curiosity acted as an elixir of relaxation for most of his guests. Watch Cavett's interview with Katherine Hepburn on YouTube, it is a master class of creating a relationship within a conversation. Hepburn settles in and literally kicks off her shoes and puts her bare feet on the coffee table.

Dick Cavett also understood the times in which he worked. He didn't shy away from the news of the day even if it didn't play well in the heartland or on the golf courses. Conversations with John Lennon, Jimi Hendrix, Angela Davis, and even a remote broadcast one summer evening in 1973 from the Senate Watergate Committee hearing room became for his audience a nightly societal Rorschach test. Cavett's was a show with purpose. In fact, I truly believe the show didn't last longer on network television because it was ridiculously ahead of its time. Outside of Norman Lear's work, much of network television in the early 1970s was still essentially escapist entertainment rooted in innocuous dramas and rimshot jokes on comedies that were safe for both grandparents and preschoolers. Cavett went on to do brilliant work years later on his PBS show where he had the time and proper platform for his brand of explorative conversation.

Dick Cavett made an indelible mark in the fiber and fabric of my internal sensitivity of what a talk show should be like, sound like, and act like. That has never wavered. Cavett is without question the best talk show host of all time.

David Letterman idolized Johnny Carson. Letterman took what Carson did, updated it, and packaged it for a new and much younger generation. Letterman has always been a broadcaster first and entertainer second. That's a compliment and a good thing. The evolution of Letterman while on NBC is pretty dramatic. In 1980's short lived and ill-fated *The David Letterman Show* and during the very early years of *Late Night with David Letterman,* Letterman was more the measured "broadcaster" who allowed the comedy bits of the show to sort of exist around him. A couple of years in, Letterman developed the "Dave" persona with the bushier hair, cigar, louder approach, and bigger personality. That's when *Letterman* became destination television, especially when it came to his interaction with guests. Dave understood that the approach needed to be much different when chatting with Madonna as opposed to talking with an 89-year-old woman from Omaha who collected balls of lint. The episode of CBS' *Late Show with David Letterman* in 2001, the first after the September 11th attacks, is the epitome of responsible entertainment and broadcast excellence.

The interviews that night were appropriately delicate and, with a couple of well-placed and much needed funny moments, Letterman told America it was alright to begin to laugh again, at least somewhat.

Letterman continued to run strong all those years at CBS and left at what many considered to be the perfect time. However, I was a bit surprised when on my show Rob Burnett, the former Executive Producer of the *Late Show with David Letterman*, told me: *To some extent, we may have stayed there a little longer than we should have. A lot of the stuff that I loved about the show, by the end, was already gone.* Either way, David Letterman left an indelible mark on the American television landscape and Dave helped cement a comedic attitude rooted in the figurative raised eyebrow that is found in the DNA of much of the comedy that has come since.

Jay Leno is a great talent and took snarky observational comedy to a more mainstream contemporary level in the early 1980s, his several appearances on *Late Night with David Letterman* were downright hysterical. Unfortunately, it turned out that Jay wasn't the best host nor the most curious interviewer. Even though he got *The Tonight Show* after Carson retired and cashed in big time as a result, I believe it stunted his overall career and eventual place in comedy history. Leno needed to curb his material and soften his look and attitude in an attempt to keep Johnny's audience and ease the transition. Rather than focusing on the twenty-somethings in the comedy clubs, he now needed to appeal to the upper end of the advertisers' preferred 25 to 54-year-old demographic upon which the 11:30 slot on NBC depended. The nightly monologues were fine and the scripted comedy pieces worked but when chatting with guests, Jay never really moved from the ask the questions from the pre-interview approach. I think Jay continued to work weekends doing stand-up during his *Tonight Show* years, so he never personally lost touch with the type of comedy and attitude that got him Carson's chair in the first place. I believe that was his way to follow his creative heart.

While I grew up in a generation that focused on television, I was always a fan of radio. There is a wonderfully intimate connection of listening to one person, a person you cannot see but is there with you. I became fascinated with who was on the other side of the speaker;

it made me wonder and it created a yearning to be on the air from a very early age. Late night radio was once magical: the wonderful snap, crackle, and pop of distant AM stations bringing in different voices and different regions of the country. As I listened in the late 1980s, two personalities left upon me an indelible mark of how a good interview and a great conversation should sound: Larry King and Tom Snyder.

Larry King was a showman, especially when he donned the suspenders and sat under the bright TV lights of CNN, but years before Ted Turner made King a television star, Larry was a street-smart radio broadcaster who understood the intimacy of talk radio and could extract more from a guest than anyone else during a long form radio interview. His overnight show, broadcast from a blue hazed, smoke-filled Mutual Radio Network studio located deep inside a rabbit warren of office buildings just across the river from Washington, DC had a personality, a feel, and a pace that no other radio talk show could match. One night it was John Dean, the next night it was Don Rickles, the next the biggest stamp collector from the Midwest: it didn't matter, King could talk with anyone, and the listener was the winner. What I learned from King is that listening is more important than talking. Lead with your ear and your curiosity and the questions will follow. Let your guest talk, let them be expressive, and then react within the conversation. Larry was his own biggest fan; that's not a terrible thing. In this business, a little hubris adds a little extra octane to the tank.

Tom Snyder crafted his reputation hosting *Tomorrow* late nights on NBC in the 1970s after Johnny Carson finished up for the evening on *The Tonight Show.* Tom was an incredibly self-confident large voiced traditional broadcaster. He seemingly spent the '70s with a lit cigarette held at attention by two fingers and his elbow poised on the armrest as he held court with authors, celebrities, and many significant newsmakers of the day. Snyder scored an interview with Charles Manson which underscored both Manson's utter madness and Snyder's ability to work as a conversational journalist in an extremely unique situation. Snyder had a way to get what he wanted and what he needed from a guest. He could ask the same question several different ways until he received the answer for which he tasked himself. That's not easy to do. NBC canceled *Tomorrow* in the fall of 1981 to make way for *Late Night with David Letterman.* Soon after, Snyder started a brief stint as a snarky local news anchor at WABC-TV in New York, then it was off to Los Angeles for a local talk show on KABC-TV. Unfortunately, it seemed as if Snyder's shelf life would hit its expiration date relatively often. Tom then headed to network radio and that's how I remember him best and what impressed me most.

Snyder's four year run on the ABC Radio Network was a late-night journey into terrific and inquisitive conversation. Tom seemed to relax on the radio and perhaps the setting of a dark radio studio with his sleeves rolled up and a jar of cashews at arm's reach allowed him to loosen up and let his personality shine. Tom had a great sense of humor. I believe this was Snyder at his apex; he was great at doing talk radio and for someone who loved broadcasting not only as a medium but as an art form, it should have been enough. But, alas, he couldn't resist the lure of a television studio. After a brief two-year-run on CNBC, Snyder was tapped by CBS (actually by David Letterman himself) for their 12:30 slot. I believe Letterman was being a bit more nostalgic than pragmatic when it came to the hiring of Snyder. Through most of the 1970s, Snyder's *Tomorrow* followed Johnny Carson's *Tonight Show.*

The deliciously romantic juxtaposition for Letterman to then have Snyder follow him in the 1990s had to be a major factor in his decision to pursue Snyder for 12:30. It always seemed to me that Letterman never really got over not getting the *Tonight Show* after Carson, thus this was a small way to recreate the NBC of the 70s on the CBS of the 90s. More troublesome was the fact that late night was beginning to skew younger and hipper and people with Snyder's talents and experience were headed to the world of cable news. Remember,

Snyder was already there at CNBC. If Snyder had stayed with CNBC instead of jumping to CBS to follow Letterman, Tom would have been in the NBC corporate family when MSNBC debuted in 1996. Snyder would have been the perfect choice to go head-to-head against Larry King on CNN. It would have kept Snyder in a more appropriate format and demographic for what he could do and I firmly feel he would have been extremely successful. Even though Snyder had his moments while hosting CBS' *The Late Late Show,* he was bogged down with too many fluff interviews with the *in* celebrities of the mid to late '90s, many of whom resided outside of Tom's personal frame of reference. After leaving the show in 1999, Snyder almost immediately faded away from the electronic public square and passed away in 2007. I always thought that even though Tom Snyder's career was brilliant on many levels, there could have and should have been more.

It was on the radio where I rediscovered someone much better remembered for his work in television: Steve Allen. WNEW AM 1130, or *Eleven-Three-Oh* as they called themselves, was on its last legs as a music station in New York in the mid-1980s when they decided to bring Allen in to host afternoon drive. What started as a mix of Allen's humor, sitting at a piano dovetailed with the songs of Frank Sinatra, Mel Torme, and Tony Bennett, evolved into a talk show which soon became syndicated around the country via the NBC Radio Network. The show was a throwback to an earlier time, a time of showbiz schmaltz that by the mid-1980s was beginning to recede within more sophisticated times. Still, the show was a fun and interesting listen. It became quite an industry encyclopedia featuring all the great comedians and comic actors who worked from the early '50s through the mid '80s. One of the more frequent guests who appeared nearly every day was actor and comedy writer Bob Einstein. Einstein remains best known to modern audiences for playing Marty Funkhouser on *Curb Your Enthusiasm.*

Years earlier, Steve Allen's place in TV history was firmly cemented after being the first host of NBC's *Tonight Show.* Allen went on to host a Sunday night primetime show opposite Ed Sullivan on CBS and then a few other shows on ABC and in syndication based within the same variety format. Allen was an extremely competent host but tended to depend a great deal on those who surrounded him. It turned Allen into a straight man for a cast of supporting character comedians such as Don Knotts, Louis Nye, Tom Poston, and Pat Harrington. Allen fit the role perfectly and his brand of humor which featured puns and plays on words was pitch perfect for the buttoned up 1950s and very early 1960s.

Allen was perhaps one of the most erudite entertainers who ever lived. Politically progressive but somewhat culturally conservative, especially when it came to entertainment, Allen wrote extensively about the world around him. He was also a voracious composer of music; in fact, his music catalog may be the most impressive element of his career.

If there was one thing which held Allen back, it was Steve Allen himself. The final third of Allen's career seemed consumed with his constant battle against what he believed was the filth and vulgarity of modern media. Allen seemed uncomfortable with the way society and the younger segment of the entertainment industry were evolving culturally in the '70s and '80s and appeared to believe that the comedy formula which worked in the tuxedo-dressed days of the '50s and '60s should still work. It didn't and Allen's days on TV became fewer and farther in between, outside of a few acting appearances always along with his wife Jayne Meadows. Even on his mid '80s radio show, Allen would ring a bell and stop a guest whenever he believed that performer was "wallowing in filth." It was commercial radio in the mid '80s, at worst what Allen was objecting to was usually a double entendre joke which had already made the rounds of every middle school playground.

I still find Allen's late career crusade against his perceived vulgarity a bit odd considering that for years on his television shows he would feature Bill Dana and his Jose Jimenez character, a character that even for its day seems bluntly offensive and downright racist. Considering Allen's political sensitivities, that choice of humor to me always seemed quite paradoxical. I guess it proves we are indeed products of the times in which we live and are shaped by the societal sensitivities of those times. But in retrospect, I find Steve Allen frustrating because here was this incredibly intelligent, witty, and socially aware man who couldn't understand why the humor of the '50s didn't play in the '80s and had a very poorly calibrated personal barometer of what was truly over the line. His syndicated radio show went off the air with little fanfare in March of 1988 and Allen quickly faded away from the relevant entertainment world. That's a shame.

The radio station that influenced me more than any other as I was growing up was 66 WNBC in New York. Yes, I was caught up in the early euphoria, which was Howard Stern, not because he was saying "bad things" on the radio, but because Stern sounded so ridiculously comfortable in front of a microphone. Here was a real guy, without the typical "announcer" voice which was still commonplace when Stern arrived in New York in 1982; he came off as being completely in tune with his audience. My affinity for WNBC from '82 until its demise on October 7, 1988, when NBC decided to vacate the radio business is rooted, not in Stern, but in what I also heard on the station.

Soupy Sales was a rimshot and sometimes corny TV comedian, game show panelist, and former kids show host who hosted middays on WNBC for a few years and did a show that was wonderfully schmaltzy and rooted in "showbiz." After Stern left WNBC in late 1985, afternoons featured Joey Reynolds, a radio veteran best known for his earlier time in Buffalo who was a lot like Soupy Sales but more of a nuts-and-bolts radio guy. If you want to hear someone hosting what was supposed to be a "fun radio show" with reverence and responsibility, listen to the aircheck of *The Joey Reynolds Show* on WNBC from October 22, 1986, when traffic reporter Jane Dornacker was killed on the air when the traffic helicopter she was broadcasting from nose-dived, hit a fence, and crashed into the Hudson River. Listen also to the aircheck from the following day as the radio station gave perspective and dignity to a personal tragedy which occurred so publicly. Reynolds, co-host Jay Sorensen, and the entire WNBC staff were brilliant.

After Reynolds left, Alan Colmes was the final afternoon drive personality on WNBC. The national audience remembers Colmes best for his long run at Fox News as co-host of *Hannity and Colmes*, but Colmes' best work came while at WNBC. Colmes was smart, a great conversationalist, funny, and a bit ahead of his times in many ways. The programmer behind the WNBC that made me want to go into radio was Dale Parsons. During this time, AM radio was in flux and most of it would soon give way to political ideologues who tended to stir up more angst than smiles. But for this short fleeting time in the '80s, Parsons guided a jewel of a radio station which bucked the trend and proved that mass appeal personality radio works and is remembered. In late 2020 as my parents packed up and moved from my childhood home, I pulled open the closet in my old bedroom one last time and saw my 35-year-old 66 WNBC Radio bumper sticker still affixed to the back of the door in perfect pristine condition, protected by three and a half decades of darkness. It read: "There's Only One Place for People Like Us: 66 WNBC."

One notable WNBC personality had his greatest success not on WNBC but on WFAN, which took over the 660 AM frequency in New York. Don Imus was a wonderful conversationalist who wasted the early part of his career talking up Fleetwood Mac records and trying to be the bad boy of radio. After his "Hey baby, how's your Donkey Kong" act grew stale and was surpassed and marginalized by Howard Stern in the late 1980s, Imus needed to reinvent himself. Imus' show became appointment radio beginning in the early 1990s and through the mid-2000s as he became the darling of the movers and shakers in both politics and media. During this time, Imus owned the attention of anyone who mattered in politics and the important news media along the Northeast Corridor from Boston through New York and down to Washington. His interviews were smart, conversational, and unafraid. He didn't fear humor, nor did he fear asking tough questions. He was "in" with both sides of the political spectrum. Many believe he was instrumental in getting Bill Clinton elected in 1992 and securing the Republican nomination for Robert Dole in 1996.

Imus was on CNN with Larry King, featured on *60 Minutes*, seemed to enjoy actual friendships with Tim Russert and John McCain, and landed on the cover of *Newsweek*. I enjoyed this reinvention of Imus but along with millions of others was disgusted when on the morning of April 4, 2007, he made his infamous racist comments about the Rutgers University women's basketball team. While Imus' conversations with his guests were always an engaging listen, much of the rest of the show often bordered on the inappropriate. Racist, sexist, and homophobic quips were commonplace with Imus' on-air crew. The Rutgers incident forced those who yearned to be an Imus guest to take a closer look at what was really being said on that show when he wasn't chatting with Joe Lieberman, Pat Buchanan, Bill Bradley, James Carville, or Mary Matalin. Outside of the interviews, much of what the Imus crew did wouldn't be tolerated today on commercial media or in our society.

I think at least for me, when listening back to twenty-five-year-old airchecks of the Imus show, outside of his interviews, it made me realize how we've evolved in what is acceptable in terms of our conversation in the so-called public square. Obviously, there exists freedom of speech which is a foundational tenet upon which our democracy is built. But freedom within a society is appropriately tethered to responsibility. We've begun to better understand that, especially over the past few years. Words mean things and they are tools which can be used for the constructive good or the destructive bad. I've always chosen to use my words within my corner of the public square in the most positive way I can.

Thus, as you can see, I've always absorbed media, literature, performance, and entertainment the way an overly porous sponge absorbs water. Not only did what I consume create an appreciation of it, but also a deep desire to be involved in it. The resulting journey has always been interesting.

That journey continues. There are so many more conversations to enjoy. Oh, and to that psychic/medium back on UBA-TV who predicted in 2009 that I would someday write a book, kudos to you.

Now, about next week's Powerball numbers...

Acknowledgements

I wrote a book. That's a short declarative sentence that summarizes several months of me sitting late-nights in front of a keyboard and, more importantly, the efforts of many others who fueled my literary fire and helped me along this journey.

I have an incredible literary agent: Diane Nine, of Nine Speakers headquartered in Washington, DC. Diane's guidance, friendship, and vision through this entire process, from concept to completion, was greatly welcomed and will always be tremendously appreciated.

My thanks to the publisher, the great team at Rand-Smith. Thank you for believing in my work and making this book a reality.

My wife Diane Kalegi, who always understood why I wanted to do what I do, never doubted my ability to do it, and with her urging and encouragement guided me to once again pursue the dream which was muted and derailed years earlier.

My son Eddie who, at the time of this writing, is a Journalism and Media Studies student at Rutgers University, the sports director at WRSU-FM, and a member of the telecast crew on Big Ten Plus. He is carving his own niche as he begins his professional journey with his dream of a career in sports media. Recently, Eddie was inducted into Kappa Tau Alpha, a college honor society which recognizes academic excellence in journalism and mass communication. He makes me prouder with each passing day.

There would be no guests, no conversations, without the constant support of the several publicists in New York, Los Angeles, and Washington who continue to show their support by placing their clients in my vocal hands. People such as Charlie Barrett, Jeff Abraham, Dan Harary, Art Sears, Peter Marchese, AJ Feuerman, Susana Franco, Angelo Ellerbe, Kevin Goins, Danny Deraney, Terry Cater, Harlan Boll, and more: ten years and a constant pipeline of interesting and entertaining people to speak with. I thank them all for their continued trust in me and value each and every one of these relationships.

Finally, my thanks to YOU. You read this book, you listen to my work wherever you are from coast to coast, around the globe, even up to the heavens. Without you there is no need for what I do and, for that, I'm eternally grateful.

About the Author

I'm Ed Kalegi. My journey began in my suburban New Jersey bedroom when I was seven years old. As other kids my age were playing with G.I.Joe, clogging the egg tray in the fridge with Play-Doh, and breaking their mom's best vase by throwing bean bags at Toss Across, I was concerned with the day-to-day operation of a radio station: my radio station. No, I wasn't a Marconi-like or Edison-ish engineering whippersnapper; I was a kid who loved listening to the radio and loved the idea of being the voice on the radio. So, there I was with a Radio Shack Walkie Talkie with the TALK button taped down so my mic would always be on, and I began a love affair that endures to this day.

I consumed American pop culture when not "broadcasting" on my walkie-talkie radio station. I watched too much TV for a kid, which was a good thing. I was especially interested in watching the art of conversation. Even as a kid, I absorbed the quick wit and artful conversational skill of Dick Cavett and the suave and sophisticated yet comedic wink in the eye of Johnny Carson. As a college student consumed with late-night talk radio, I marveled at the ability of Larry King and Tom Snyder to create an intimacy between host and guest, which branded an indelible mark upon my conversational soul.

As a student at Rutgers University, my curiosities increased as I began to explore a career in media. My first on-air experiences occurred at the two campus radio stations, where I hosted both a morning and late-night talk show. It proved to be both a wonderful and educational experience as the show grew in popularity and celebrities such as comedian Gilbert Gottfried and Green Party Presidential Candidate Ralph Nader dropped by the show.

After college, my immediate professional journey led me to a position as branch manager of a local marketing firm, and then to own my own souvenir clothing and promotional products company aimed at nursery schools and daycare centers. However, the itch had not been scratched. I longed to be on the air and decided that my future and my talents were both better off in the media, and thus, the pursuit began.

The early years were eclectic: check out some old episodes of *Law and Order* and *Law and Order: SVU*; you might see me in the background as a befuddled cop fiddling at a broken coffee machine, perhaps as a detective rushing through the station house carrying an empty file folder in a hectic rush to the other side of the room, maybe even as a CSI tech meticulously picking up the evidence with tweezers but really more concerned with whether or not I'll make the last train out of Penn Station to New Jersey that night.

Other early jobs in "the business" included a handful of commercial voiceovers, recording nightly forecasts for Weather Phone, a five-year stint as the stadium announcer for the New York Yankees' minor league team in Staten Island, a three-year hitch as the backup arena announcer for the New Jersey Devils, and a long run as a radio news, weather, and traffic reporter in New York City. "Hey, New York, guess what? Traffic on the BQE is slow." It's always slow, even at 3 AM on a Sunday.

But during this time, I kept harkening back to what I was exposed to while growing up: all those nights watching Cavett and Carson and listening to King and Snyder. I wanted more. I wanted *that.* I wanted to do what I truly believed I was always meant to do: host my own talk show. There was no turning back; as Ed Harris says in *Apollo 13*: "Failure is not an option."

In July of 2014, the itch was finally scratched, and the quest was finally rewarded. *America Weekend with Ed Kalegi* debuted and syndicated to 35 stations across America. It felt great, but one thing would make it perfect: I wanted Dick Cavett on the show. I put the word out to the interns and the network to see if we could somehow get Dick on the show. At some point, I figured he'd agree to chat for a few minutes.

It took only three weeks. I chatted with Dick for a half-hour on the show, my show. Now it was perfect.

Through the years, the show has evolved into *The Weekend with Ed Kalegi,* and I've had the pleasure of speaking with dozens and dozens of actors, music artists, journalists, authors, difference makers, and noted experts. I do my own research for each one, my inherent curiosity is my compass. The result has been a full and continuously growing catalog of aural portraits of interesting people. The time has come to share them once again in written form.

Milton Keynes UK
Ingram Content Group UK Ltd.
UKHW031618231124
451036UK00004B/56